# On Nuclear War and Peace

## Albert Schweitzer

### Edited by Homer A. Jack

*Preface by*

*Rhena Schweitzer Miller*

BRETHREN PRESS
Elgin, Illinois

## On Nuclear War and Peace

Copyright © 1988 by Homer A. Jack

BRETHREN PRESS, 1451 Dundee Avenue, Elgin, IL 60120.

Cover design by Ken Stanley

The editor and publisher wish to thank the holders of copyrighted materials for permission to publish in this collection selected writings by Albert Schweitzer.

Published in cooperation with Albert Schweitzer Fellowship, 866 United Nations Plaza, New York, NY 10017

**Library of Congress Cataloging in Publication Data**

Schweitzer, Albert, 1875-1965.
    (Selections. 1987)
    On nuclear war and peace / Albert Schweitzer; edited by Homer A. Jack, with a preface by Rhena Schweitzer Miller.
        P.    cm.
    Bibliography: p.
    Includes index.
    ISBN 0-87178-536-6
    1. Nuclear warfare—Moral and ethical aspects.
    2. Peace.
    I. Title
    U263.S39A2 1987
    172' . 42—dc19

Manufactured in the United States of America

# Contents

## *Addresses*

## *Letters*

## *Legacy*

# Preface

Today, with the threat of nuclear war becoming ever more real and frightening, it is fitting to remember that 30 years ago, from his hospital in the forests of Equatorial Africa, my father Albert Schweitzer spoke out vigorously and prophetically against the dangers of nuclear weapons and testing. The predominant view at the time minimized, or did not even recognize, these dangers.

Forty years before that, at the time of World War I, my father's deep concern that our technological civilization did not possess a valid ethical basis led him to propose that such an ethic could be found in the moral imperative of Reverence for Life. He discovered this concept during a trip on the majestic River Ogowé to visit a patient in the African jungle.

From that time on, Reverence for Life guided Albert Schweitzer in all that he thought and undertook. However, until the ninth decade of his life, he did not feel that he should speak out on matters construed to be of a political nature. Efforts to persuade him to lend his voice and moral stature to the campaign against nuclear weapons during the first decade after the bombing of Hiroshima and Nagasaki were unsuccessful.

Albert Schweitzer's acceptance speech for the award of the 1952 Nobel Peace Prize mentioned only briefly, and in general terms, the dangers of nuclear war. But in 1957, after Norman Cousins' persuasive visit to the Schweitzer Hospital in Lambaréné, my father finally became convinced that he should join with such leaders as Albert Einstein, Bertrand

Russell, and Linus Pauling in trying to inform and arouse public opinion on the danger and the folly of nuclear armaments and nuclear testing.

My father felt strongly that he must first inform himself on the technical details and health consequences of nuclear radiation. Only then could he address himself clearly to the common man in behalf of human rights. He thought that stirring up public opinion and making people aware that their rights and international law were being violated would be the most effective way to fight against the atomic danger. I know at first hand what a great deal of time and energy my father devoted to this effort, from his eightieth to ninetieth year. In addition he continued his close supervision of the Lambaréné hospital, a task which most men half his age would find completely exhausting.

Speaking out for sanity in nuclear arms policy in the 1950s and 1960s required great courage. These were the years of McCarthyism, which was not limited to North America, and backyard bomb shelters. Many moderate and responsible voices were labeled communist automatically if they dared to question the buildup and testing of nuclear arms. My father suffered this fate, and much of the mounting criticism of his hospital during this period seemed designed to discredit him as a critic of nuclear arms testing. But he persisted undeterred, with increased concern that he gain greater command of the technical facts of nuclear energy in order to strengthen his words. Until his last days, he spared no time or effort in this battle, feeling even then that despite all his endeavors he had not done enough.

Homer Jack first visited my father at Lambaréné in the early 1950s. Working with Norman Cousins, he too is one of the far-sighted persons who has long recognized the nuclear danger and realized how important it is to stem it through nuclear disarmament. He spent almost a quarter of a century in the United Nations community advocating disarmament on behalf of a number of world religious organizations.

In 1977, at the Albert Schweitzer Symposium in Wingspread, Wisconsin, Homer Jack spoke about my father's thought

thought and its relationship to the contemporary scene. Now he has revised and enlarged this presentation to its present form. I am most grateful to Dr. Jack for putting together these documents of my father and reminding us in his essay of the escalation of nuclear armaments and testing. I consider this publication at this time most important and relevant. Never before has the danger of nuclear annihilation of our world and our civilization been greater. My father in his time had done his best to fight it. May his voice and the voices of all concerned people be heard and heeded.

*Rhena Schweitzer Miller*
*Lavonia, Georgia*

# Introduction
## *Albert Schweitzer's Activism in Nuclear Politics*[1]
### Homer A. Jack

Albert Schweitzer lived for two full decades into the atomic age, yet he became impelled to study and act on the issues of nuclear politics only in the second decade of this era—1955 through 1965. This period which coincided with the ninth and final decade of his life began between the announcement of the award of the 1952 Nobel Peace Prize in 1953 and after his acceptance of the honor in Oslo, Norway in 1954. At that time in life when most human beings become physically and mentally less active, and often more conservative, Schweitzer in his eighties was growing in knowledge and activism about peace, disarmament, and nuclear weapons tests.

In the first decade after World War II, Schweitzer became a world-acclaimed figure, yet he refused repeatedly to use his accelerating fame for "political" ends. As more honors were given to Schweitzer and he was stimulated by the international press to respond publicly to them, he still hesitated to go beyond delivering his philosophical, non-activist views.

An example of this attitude was his acceptance speech for the Peace Prize of the German Book Trade Association at Frankfurt on September 16, 1951.[2] He had previously officially visited that city in 1932 in the midst of rising Hitlerism to observe the centenary of Goethe's death. Two decades later, a prize was presented to him by President Theodor Heuss of the Federal Republic of Germany whose marriage Schweitzer had performed in 1908. In the acceptance address Schweitzer did not mention atomic weapons once, although he did acknow-

ledge that "the fate of mankind is in the balance." In this
address he reflected and refined his philosophy of history and
civilization—a continuation of his earlier writings. Those who
even then looked to Schweitzer to discuss contemporary
issues or to become "political" remained disappointed.

*By the end of 1951—the year Schweitzer received the Ger-
man Peace Prize—two nations had exploded a total of 27
nuclear weapons in testing or warfare (including the bombing
of Hiroshima and Nagasaki) since 1945: 24 by the United States
and three by the Soviet Union. Six years into the atomic era, the
genie was only slowly being tested out of the bottle.[3] The United
Nations established in 1946, through the first resolution adopted
by the General Assembly, an Atomic Energy Commission. Composed of all members of the Security Council and Canada, this
Commission was to deal with atomic weapons. It accomplished
almost nothing.*

THE NOBEL PRIZE
　　In October 1953, the Nobel Committee in Oslo, Norway,
announced that Schweitzer would become the Nobel Peace
Prize laureate for 1952. (While the other four Nobel prizes are
awarded from Sweden, a special committee of the Norwegian
Parliament—Storting—determines the peace prize laureate.)
The deliberations of the committee were confidential, but it
was known that the pressures in the early 1950s within Scan-
dinavia to give a Nobel prize to Schweitzer were abundant.
Many felt that he deserved a prize among one of the five Nobel
categories—medicine or physiology, chemistry, physics,
literature, and peace—and those concerned may have concluded that he most closely fit the "peace" designation. Such
may also have been the thinking of Max Tau, a German who fled
Nazism for Norway. A writer and publisher, Tau remained in
Norway after the end of World War II and his was one private
initiative in proposing that Schweitzer receive the peace
prize.
　　Schweitzer received news of the award in Africa. He could
not leave his work at his hospital to journey to Europe to
receive the prize in 1953. At the award ceremony on October
30th, Gunnar Jahn, head of the Nobel Committee in Oslo,

delivered an address about Schweitzer. The French Ambassador, M. de Monicault, was authorized by Schweitzer to accept the medal and citation. It was understood that Schweitzer would deliver his acceptance address on another occasion. The funds received for the prize ($36,000) Schweitzer used immediately to begin construction of a leper village adjoining the hospital.

Even before Schweitzer went to Europe in May 1954 to accept the Nobel Prize, he did "speak out" on nuclear issues—once. The *Daily Herald* of London asked for his comments on a proposal by professor Alexander Haddow that the United Nations should convene a conference of scientists on the hydrogen bomb. Acting out of character, Schweitzer responded to this journalistic enterprise and wrote a short essay which was printed, in full, in the *Daily Herald* on April 14th, together with his photograph, autograph, and biography under the heading: "The H-Bomb: There is Anguish in My Heart, Says Dr. Albert Schweitzer." In this article, he minimized the effectiveness of conferences—"there are too many conferences in the world today"—but he urged individual scientists, singly and in groups, to speak out. This plea anticipated his later strategy on changing governmental policy on nuclear issues.[4]

Schweitzer's letter in the *Daily Herald* was read by a young French atomic scientist, Noel Martin. This stimulated him to publish a communication to the Academy of Sciences in Paris on the effects of atomic radiation. He said that hydrogen bombs were "terrible and inadmissible death-dealing machines" and their use would result in "numerous irreversible and cumulative phenomena, which will irremediably affect the existence of life." With the world press clamoring for more material on atomic radiation, Mr. Martin corresponded with Schweitzer in December 1954, asking him to write the preface to a book he was finishing. However, Schweitzer refused to do so on the grounds that he did not wish to become involved in an issue about which he was not qualified to speak. (Later, Martin wrote Schweitzer that he had been dismissed from his post at the French National Center of Scientific Research for publicizing his findings; even obtaining his doctorate was now in jeopardy.)[5]

Schweitzer was, at that time, especially cautious because he was being criticized by his friends over a controversy of his own making. He agreed to become an honorary patron of a German youth organization working for peace which was, however, communist. The criticism became so severe that Schweitzer finally withdrew his patronage, learning belatedly that his name would be widely used for all kinds of political purposes.[6]

Going to Europe in May 1954, Schweitzer worked on his acceptance speech to be given in Oslo on November fourth. Enroute by train from his European home in Günsbach, he was treated by the public as if he were a movie star. He travelled first class, at the insistence of the Nobel Committee, and he commented about his Oslo hotel: "What do I need running water for? Am I a trout?" So many people desired to greet Schweitzer that a Norwegian newspaper suggested that everyone who wanted to shake hands with him should instead give a krone to his hospital. As a result, the amount given to him by the Nobel Committee was doubled.[7]

Friends urged Schweitzer to take the rare opportunity of his Nobel address to shock the world out of a lethargy which accepted atomic tests and even the prospect of atomic war. Yet Schweitzer was not ready to break with his European academic tradition and his own inclinations. He constructed his address carefully, recalling that "I worked almost half a year on the Nobel acceptance speech."[8] Just before delivering the address, he was told that he had to cut its length more than one-half to 35 minutes. He later told Norman Cousins that "for a moment, just before I got up to speak, I was tempted to reach for the full message even at the risk of being stopped halfway through my speech. But I downed the temptation out of courtesy to my hosts."[9]

Schweitzer delivered his acceptance address on November 4th.[10] The distinguished audience included King Gustav Adolf, Schweitzer's wife and daughter, and many friends and co-workers. He spoke in French. Charles Joy wrote afterwards: "Dr. Schweitzer was not an effective speaker with his manuscript. He seldom looked up from it; his voice was not strong and had little resonance; his inflections were regular and monotonous. The occasion was too important for extemporaneous utterance, but Dr. Schweitzer would have made a much more dynamic impression if he had spoken directly from the heart."[11] What Schweitzer wrote was, at the time, vintage Schweitzer, interwoven with history, philosophy, ethics, and religion. He did mention nuclear politics, but not extensively. He did assert that large-scale atomic "experiments might provoke a catastrophe that would endanger the very existence of humanity." He added that "we can no longer evade the problem of the future of our race."

*By the end of 1954 there were a total of 68 nuclear explosions by three nations: 51 by the United States, 14 by the Soviet Union, and three by the United Kingdom. One of these explosions was from a U.S. hydrogen bomb detonated on March 1st at the Bikini Atoll in the South Pacific. The fallout on the crew of the "Lucky Dragon" alerted the world to the dangers of radioactivity and caused Indian Prime Minister Jawaharlal Nehru on April 2nd to call for a "standstill agreement" on testing. In the meantime, the United Nations established a Disarmament Commission to deal with these matters.*

RESISTING PRESSURES

Schweitzer took very seriously the meaning of his being a-warded the Nobel Peace Prize. He resolved to fit into the shoes of the handful of peace laureates then alive—such as Ralph Bunche, Lord Boyd-Orr, Viscount Cecil, and John R. Mott—and such deceased ones as Jane Addams, Fridtjof Nansen, and Woodrow Wilson. Schweitzer was quoted as saying: "They gave me the Peace Prize—I don't know why. Now I feel I should do something to earn it."[12] But he carefully considered the several options available to him.

In December 1954 Schweitzer went from Günsbach on his eleventh sojourn to Africa, arriving just before his eightieth birthday observance on January 14, 1955. One of the many tributes he received in Africa was a message from Albert Einstein printed in an American-edited *Festschrift*.[13] On February 20th, Schweitzer responded by letter to the words of Einstein. He thanked Einstein, but then showed concern about a new series of nuclear weapons tests. He revealed that both were receiving letters that they should together speak out and demand action from the UN Schweitzer wrote that he realized that the world organization was an autonomous body, but still he wondered why its members could not "rise to the occasion."[14] Einstein never replied, since he died a few weeks later—on April 18th.[15]

Dag Hammarskjöld, Secretary-General of the United Nations, had occasion in a letter to Schweitzer to congratulate him for the Nobel Prize: "The Nobel Institute has acted with great discernment; no man of the present day has contributed more than you have to the development of the spiritual conditions required for world brotherhood and a lasting peace."[16] Then in July 1955, Hammarskjöld wrote to Schweitzer again, urging him to speak out:

You know, as I do, that the world absolutely needs an ideology which can confer a valid meaning to the efforts of all nations and give fresh and solid bases to the principle of "co-existence."

Thus, I am persuaded that it behooves you, even within the strictly political field that concerns the UN, to send forth an essential message to the world. I have already had an opportunity to tell you that in my opinion it would be possible to animate international life with a new spirit by making better known the very attitude that you have tried to explain to the men of our generation. It is precisely for this reason that we at the U.N. have contracted a debt of gratitude to you for what you have done and what you symbolize; but this is also why we make bold to hope that you will perhaps choose to add your powerful voice to the appeals made in favor of mutual respect among nations, in the very sense that we understand this term at the U.N.[17]

In July 1955, Schweitzer was back in Europe. One of the few "conferences" he attended was in this period. Almost as soon as he landed, he went to Lindau, Germany, on Lake Constance, to meet with some Nobel laureates who were convening for the third consecutive year. The group issued an appeal declaring that "a nation that engages in total war thus signals its own destruction and imperils the whole world." This was released on July 15th, only a few days after the Einstein-Russell Manifesto on atomic issues was issued in London. The Landau appeal was signed by a number of laureates, both present and

absent, but not by Schweitzer even though he was present.[18]
In Europe, Schweitzer accepted many honors. While in London in October to receive the Order of Merit from the Queen at Buckingham Palace, he met Bertrand Russell for the first time. They spoke only briefly, but this encounter began an exchange of letters which—over a decade—helped change Schweitzer's approach to contemporary political issues, including disarmament.[19]

Several months earlier, Russell had released to the press the Einstein-Russell Manifesto which Einstein signed a few days before his death in April. Schweitzer was not a co-signer. He was not invited to do so, although in a letter to Russell in March, Einstein wrote that "it would be highly desirable to have Albert Schweitzer join our group."[20] Perhaps it was this recommendation which encouraged Russell a few months later to meet Schweitzer and immediately discuss atomic issues. Schweitzer started their decade-long correspondence, but it was not until 1957 that Schweitzer wrote him for the second time.

Schweitzer returned to Africa in December 1955 for his twelfth sojourn and remained there for the entire year of 1956. Not too much is known about his thoughts during that year, except that he may have been preparing himself for a much more politically active year in 1957.

*In July 1955 there was a Summit conference at Geneva involving President Dwight Eisenhower, Premier Nikita Khrushchev, and the leaders of the United Kingdom and France. In 1956 Adlai E. Stevenson made his second unsuccessful bid for the American presidency, raising the nuclear testing issue. In the meantime, by the end of 1956, in a two-year period, the United States tested 36 additional nuclear weapons, the Soviet Union fourteen, and the United Kingdom six. Also a five-nation sub-committee of the United Nations Disarmament Commission explored the elements of a test-ban treaty in London in March-May 1956.*

LISTENING
    The indirect influences on Schweitzer to speak out on atomic issues were accumulating. Peer pressure mounted.

Before Einstein died, Schweitzer in 1954 wrote: "Just look at the influence Einstein has, because of the anguish he shows in the face of the atomic bomb."[21] Also the activity of Bertrand Russell on nuclear politics affected Schweitzer deeply, although they did not correspond between late 1955 and Schweitzer's letter to him on the last day of 1957. In it Schweitzer attached "much importance" to Russell's helping to arrange what became the first Pugwash conference of scientists. Schweitzer also commended Russell for his open letter to both President Eisenhower and Premier Khrushchev, dated November 1957, in which Russell addressed both as "most potent sirs" and reminded them that their countries had far more in common than differences. Schweitzer congratulated Russell "for using your authority in this way."[22]

Still a third instance of peer pressure was from Pablo Casals, the musician. Schweitzer once chided his friend, Casals, for the latter's controversial public utterances. Schweitzer at the time insisted that it was better to create than to protest. "No," Casals replied, "there are times when the only creative thing we can do is to protest; we must refuse to accept or acknowledge what is evil or wicked." Later, when Schweitzer did protest nuclear tests, Casals commented: "I am glad my old friend is protesting too against nuclear weapons tests."[23]

Then the American editor and critic, Norman Cousins entered the scene. He arrived at Lambaréné early in January 1957, accompanied by Mrs. Clara Urquhart, an English woman who was much more than an interpreter. A friend of both Schweitzer and Cousins, she played a useful role as an aide to the former on several occasions, including the trip to Oslo. One of the purposes of Cousins' trip was to urge Schweitzer to make some statement on world peace and atomic tests. In their initial conversation at Lambaréné on this topic, Schweitzer indicated that his concern about atomic matters had increased when he met with some of the Nobel laureates at Landau in 1955. Many spoke with urgency and gravity about the growing atomic problem. Alongside the problem of peace, everything seemed small. Schweitzer felt that a very high order of public understanding was necessary to deal with peace. "It is a serious thing that the governments have supplied so little information to their people on this subject." Cousins responded that it was precisely Schweitzer who could educate the world public. He was among the very few individuals in the world who would have an audience for anything he might say. Yet Schweitzer, several years even after delivering his Nobel address, responded: "All my life I have carefully stayed away from making pronouncements on public matters. Groups would come to me for my views on certain political questions. And always I would feel forced to say no." Schweitzer added: "It was not because I had no interest in world affairs or politics . . . It was just that I felt that my connection with the outside world should grow out of my work or thought in the field of theology or philosophy or music. I have tried to relate myself to the problems of all humankind rather than to become involved in disputes between this or that group. I wanted to be one man speaking to another man."

Thus Schweitzer insisted to Cousins that he was not the person to educate the world on atomic issues, even though the world admittedly had to be educated in lieu of the governments doing the task. He said that it was really a problem for scientists. It would be too easy to discredit any nonscientist, including himself, who spoke out on this topic. He doubted the propriety of his making any statement.[24]

Cousins persisted and the next day Schweitzer seemed more agreeable to working on some "declaration or statement or whatever it is you want to call it." Schweitzer had no reason to believe that anything he might do or say "would or should have any substantial effect." But if there were "even the smallest usefulness that I or anyone else might have on this question, it would seem almost mandatory that the effort be made." Then Schweitzer discussed the parameters of any statement. One addressing itself to the dangers and consequences of war would be too broad. Perhaps "the place to take hold is with the matter of nuclear testing." He felt that "the scientific aspects of testing may be complicated, but the issues involved in testing are not." He was inclined to settle for "a fairly limited objective." Then they reviewed how the statement might best be issued. Cousins felt a statement could be released to the news agencies. Schweitzer had little faith in the press, but concluded that "our first job is to bring the baby into the world." Schweitzer confessed that Cousins and Urquhart, in coming to Lambaréné, "had broken down my resolve not to involve myself in anything remotely concerned with political matters." Yet the problem goes "beyond politics; it affects all men." He felt that any statement "should above all be simple and direct," not "ponderous or academic."[25]

During the talks, Schweitzer asked Cousins if the latter had brought any documentary material with him. He also asked Cousins to write a summary of facts on the question of nuclear fallout, using the reports he brought with him. In the final conversation on this subject, Schweitzer told Cousins that he wanted to make the statement as clear and complete as was humanly possible, regardless of the length. He did not want to be criticized for "leaving large gaps in the argument." He did not want to produce a truncated manuscript as he had suddenly to do with his Nobel address. He would study Cousins' material, correspond with some experts—the names of some whom Cousins gave him—and others whom he knew from the Landau meeting.[26]

The jungle conversations on this topic ended with Schweitzer writing a letter to President Eisenhower in answer to one which the American President sent to him by way of Cousins. Schweitzer wrote that in his heart "I carry the hope I may somehow be able to contribute to the peace of the world." He asserted that "we both share the conviction that humanity must find a way to control the weapons which now menace the very existence of life on earth." Choosing his words carefully, Schweitzer also wrote: "May it be given to us both to see the day when the world's peoples will realize that the fate of all humanity is now at stake, and that it is urgently necessary to make the bold decisions that can deal adequately with the agonizing situation in which the world now finds itself."[27]

Almost overnight Schweitzer became the recipient, even in Lambaréné, of a stimulating dialogue on atomic matters. Prominent intellectual leaders were corresponding with Schweitzer, some old friends, others new: Martin Buber, J. Robert Oppenheimer, Pere Dominique Pire, Aneurin Bevin, and many others. Some made the long journey to Lambaréné.

Marshall and Poling describe the situation aptly: "The visitors came to see Schweitzer as students to learn; as promoters to enlist; as politicians to exploit; as journalists to profit; as thinkers to probe; and as sceptics to be convinced."[28]

## THE DECLARATION OF CONSCIENCE

Between the time that Norman Cousins left Lambaréné on January 12, 1957, and when Schweitzer released a major statement in Oslo on April 23rd, there was much activity. Cousins returned to the United States via the Middle East and in Israel he talked to Martin Buber about his visit to Schweitzer.[29] On February 13th, Cousins wrote to his friend, Indian Prime Minister Jawaharlal Nehru, discussing his visit to Lambaréné. He asked Nehru if a meeting of world leaders in Vienna, presided over by Schweitzer, might be useful to stop nuclear weapons tests.[30] Nehru quickly replied that he doubted "if there is anyone in the world today whose opinion can carry more weight in these matters than Dr. Schweitzer." Nehru added: "No one can accuse him of partiality, and whatever he says will at least command world attention. I welcome, therefore, his intention to try his utmost to deal with the present crisis." Elsewhere in the long letter Nehru wrote: "Anyhow, Dr. Schweitzer is the one man who can take the lead." As for strategy and tactics, Nehru said: "I would like Dr. Schweitzer to trust his own judgment or, if I may use Gandhiji's phrase, his 'inner voice,' since that will be a better guide than anything that I can say."[31]

Schweitzer in a letter to Cousins, dated February 23rd, vetoed any meeting of the world leaders, since it was "much too complicated." So he "returned" to the idea of writing a message to be broadcast by radio. He asked the rhetorical question in this letter: "But to which radio can the mission of the publication be charged, without others feeling indisposed?" Then he responded to his own question: "Answer: Radio Oslo, of the city of the Nobel Peace Prize!" Leaning heavily on Cousins, Schweitzer ended his letter thus: "If you approve of it [the Oslo broadcast], please cable me 'Hospital Schweitzer Lambaréné. Agree with you.' You can cable in English. . . . But all this remains between you and me."[32] Cousins immediately responded affirmatively, sending a copy of Nehru's letter to Lambaréné.

Nehru, although governing a subcontinent, was not too busy to continue writing long, discursive letters to Cousins. On March 16th, Nehru wrote: "I entirely agree that Oslo will be the right and appropriate place for an appeal by Dr. Schweitzer, and it would certainly add to the value of the appeal for peace if it was made under the auspices of the Nobel Committee."[33]

The Nobel Committee, through its President, Gunnar Jahn, and the Director of Radio Oslo cooperated completely and arrangements were quickly made. Schweitzer wanted ample air time "to develop the facts very carefully. I don't want to be criticized for leaving large gaps in the argument." On the other hand, he wrote, "Don't ask me to come to the microphone myself."[34] In the end, it was agreed that Mr. Jahn would read the text in Norwegian, with the Declaration in other European languages—English, French, German, and Russian—being broadcast from Oslo later the same evening. Radio Oslo hoped for a date in May to broadcast the statement, but Schweitzer cabled that it would be "too late." He wanted the broadcast to coincide with a major campaign against nuclear tests which he knew would take place in the Federal Republic of Germany around April 20th.[35]

In this manner, what became known as the "Declaration of Conscience" was broadcast on April 23, 1957 and released to the world press the next day. It was widely reprinted.[36] In a letter to Cousins, written actually a day before the broadcast, Schweitzer wrote that "what's essential is that what was due to your initiative has succeeded and that the attempt to awaken the attention of humanity . . . is being undertaken under the best of conditions."[37] In another letter written to Cousins early in May, Schweitzer reported that the statement was aired from 150 transmitters throughout the world. He again acknowledged his debt to Cousins: "Without your coming here I don't think I should have decided to make the statement. You were right to encourage me to do it. I will not forget that." But pressing on, Schweitzer added: "If you have anything interesting about the nuclear situation please send it on to me. You can write in English. I can read it well."[38]

The response to the broadcast was widespread, if often intangible. Dr. Willard Libby, an American scientist who was a member of the Atomic Energy Commission, wrote Schweitzer an open letter, claiming the radiation involved in nuclear weapons tests was insignificant compared to normal quantities from other sources.[39] But a more positive result of the broadcast was that individuals on both sides of the Atlantic were becoming much more concerned and militant, making their first tentative plans to establish citizens' movements against nuclear tests. These beginnings led later in the year to the formation of the National Committee for a Sane Nuclear Policy in the United States—with Norman Cousins as one cochairman—and of the Campaign for Nuclear Disarmament (CND) in England. Both organizations are still in existence. Prime Minister Nehru in a letter to Cousins on June 6th wrote: "I agree with you that there is now a far greater realization all over the world of the effect of these test explosions than there was previously. I am sure that Schweitzer's statement has helped in this process."[40]

One person reached by the Declaration was Adlai E. Stevenson. In 1956, Schweitzer wrote Stevenson, when the American was running for the second time for President, that "I read with great interest everything that concerns you, and I admire your courage in throwing yourself again into the electoral struggle."[41] In June 1957, Stevenson visited Lambaréné. During their conversation, Stevenson filled 12 half-sheets of paper with notes on everything from philosophy to hydrogen bombs.[42] Soon after leaving Lambaréné, Stevenson issued a formal statement:

Dr. Schweitzer is gratified by the world's reception of his Declaration in April on the dangers of testing atomic devices. Heretofore man has had to obey nature. But now he has learned how to subjugate nature and Dr. Schweitzer considers this the most dangerous period in history. He commented that his views were not as widely reported in the U.S., Britain, and France as elsewhere. But he feels that his Declaration may have encouraged scientists to express their views more freely, and he was much pleased by the recent petition signed by 2,000 American scientists calling for an end of nuclear bomb tests. His information agrees with the reports I brought him, and he feels that public opinion, led by scientists who know the facts, is now moving rapidly in the right direction and will soon influence governments. He sees the issue of nuclear tests as a challenge to moral forces in the world. In that connection he detects some hopeful signs of a new spiritual awakening, and that the spirit of a true culture based on human concern for one's own life and for the life of everything that lives is increasing.[43]

In June 1957, Schweitzer went to Europe and stayed there until December. He visited Switzerland and Germany, from his headquarters in Günsbach, and he accumulated additional information on nuclear issues. Schweitzer wrote an American friend, Jerome Hill, that Erica Anderson—also an American friend—was "cutting out interesting articles and making a packet every day" regarding "the news about the danger of radioactivity in the newspapers, and the journals in German, French, and in particular English and American." Schweitzer admitted that he had to "stay up to date on this question." As a consequence he was familiar with "the results or non-results of all the congresses and the discussions exchanged between the East and the West bloc and I can judge what point the situation has reached."[44]

Writing a short letter to Cousins from Günsbach on October 14th, Schweitzer complained about the speech United States Ambassador Henry Cabot Lodge made at the United Nations minimizing the dangers of nuclear tests.[45] In another letter to Cousins, presumably written while still in Europe, Schweitzer discussed creating a worldwide movement against nuclear tests. He wrote: "The fire must be lighted in the U.S.A., and I will then be able to help other men of other lands to bring the wood to throw onto the fire and give it the importance it should have to enable it to create a different atmosphere."[46]

In this period, Schweitzer took a public position on two other international issues, both African. One was the freedom of Algeria and, some years later (in 1963), the relation of the Katanga area to the former Belgian Congo. A discussion of these two issues lies outside the purview of this volume, but merits a parallel study on Schweitzer's thinking and more hesitant action on African issues.

*The year 1957 was a banner one for activity by Schweitzer and many others against nuclear weapons tests. Yet more tests were conducted in 1957 than in any previous year: a total of 54. These included 32 by the United States, 15 by the Soviet Union,*

*and seven by the United Kingdom. In London, the United*
*Nations Disarmament Sub-Commission held meetings for five*
*months, but no agreements were made.*

THREE APPEALS

Back in Lambaréné for Christmas 1957, Schweitzer
received from American scientist Linus Pauling a request for
his signature to an appeal by scientists of many countries urging an international agreement to stop nuclear weapons tests.
Schweitzer signed the petition, along with 36 other Nobel
laureates and over 9,000 other scientists.[47]

While still in Europe, Schweitzer met Kaare Fostervoll of
Radio Oslo—in Basel, where Schweitzer had gone to purchase
medicines. They spoke of another broadcast on nuclear issues.
In February 1958, Schweitzer wrote Oslo: "Since October I
have spent the greater part of my time in keeping myself
informed about the progress of atomic weapons, and I am in
touch with experts on the subject."[48]

On April 14th, Schweitzer informed Cousins that he
finished drafting three successive appeals and that they would
be broadcast over Radio Oslo on April 28, 29, and 30. More
militant every month, Schweitzer wrote Cousins that "the text
is intended for Europe where we have to keep the NATO
generals from forcing launching pads and nuclear weapons on
the governments."[49]

The three appeals were broadcast as planned and again
made various echoes around the world.[50] They were soon
widely published as a pamphlet or small booklet under the title,
*Peace or Atomic War?* Writing to Cousins several weeks later,
Schweitzer confessed that "I am still very tired by the work on
the three appeals [and] my eyes have suffered from this." He
boasted that, because of Radio Oslo, "the whole enterprise did
not cost a cent. It is incredible."[51]

Already Schweitzer was thinking about new campaigns.
Cousins had written him on May 9th, asking about an appeal to
the World Court, signed by Pope Pius XII and himself, urging
that highest judicial body to outlaw nuclear weapons tests.
However, Schweitzer would not agree to the strategy, including an appeal to the Vatican: "Also the Pope we will leave alone.

. . . He may be a good man, but he is no fighter. Or did you ever read anywhere that he condemned the atomic and H bombs in the name of Christian religion? Protestantism does it, but there is no Catholic declaration so far. . . ." He urged that people repeat that "atomic weapons contradict international law," but without appealing to the courts directly. "We don't need the lawyers' blessings." In a postscript, he gave his philosophy on alerting public opinion: "Radio and the press are the small firewood to kindle a fire; booklets which are passed from one hand to the next are the big logs to keep the fire burning and to bring it to its full effect."[52]

TEST MORATORIUM
    *The Soviet Union on March 31, 1958 announced that it would stop all nuclear weapons tests, hoping that the United States and the United Kingdom might reciprocate. On July 1st, a conference began at Geneva between the U.S. and the U.S.S.R. and some of their allies, on verification to prevent violations of any nuclear weapons test-ban treaty. The day after this conference made its unanimous, affirmative report, in late August, President Eisenhower suggested that the Soviet Union, United Kingdom, and the United States—then the three nuclear weapons-possessing states—negotiate an agreement prohibiting all nuclear weapons tests. Further, the President announced that the U.S. would suspend testing, "on a basis of reciprocity," on a year-to-year basis, with certain provisions. The moratorium would start on October 31st when the conference at Geneva on the actual negotiations for a treaty would begin. In the meantime, the Soviet Union resumed its tests on September 1st.*

    In August, Cousins cabled Schweitzer the news that the U.S. was suspending nuclear testing. On August 24th, Schweitzer wrote a long letter to Cousins summarizing his efforts which, in one sense, culminated in the action of President Eisenhower to halt tests. Schweitzer commented: "How sad, though, that it took so long for these two states [the U.S. and the U.K.] to come to this conclusion!" In a postscript, Schweitzer added: "When I received your telegram, I thought of Einstein—what it would have meant to him if he could have lived to see the day which he longed for so much!"[53]

Pablo Casals gave a speech to the UN community in October 1958. He mentioned atomic issues and quoted Schweitzer. He sent a letter to him about the experience and enclosed his speech. Schweitzer responded on November 22nd, commenting that "never would I have imagined that you would become advocate and orator of this cause." He said: "It is a miracle that they let you pronounce the word 'atomic' at all." Again, Schweitzer directly attacked the Western governments: "There exists the great danger that the pro-atomic governments may give the impression that they search for the same thing as we do, when fundamentally they pursue nothing but to sabotage all that precisely can be done for peace in our day." Schweitzer closed by declaring: "Never, in our earlier meetings in Europe, would we have imagined that one day we would together descend in the world arena to fight against those who constitute the greatest danger for mankind of the whole world."[54]

On November 22, 1958, *The Saturday Review* published an open letter "to the men at Geneva" who were negotiating a nuclear test-ban agreement. Schweitzer led the list of 16 persons who endorsed it. Others included Toyohiko Kagawa of Japan, Trygve Lie of Norway, Gunnar Myrdal of Sweden, Martin Niemoeller of the German Federal Republic, C. Rajagopalachari of India, Mrs. Eleanor Roosevelt, and Bertrand Russell of the United Kingdom.[55] On November 24th, Schweitzer wrote Cousins thanking him for taking the initiative with the open letter. He concluded that "despite all the political happenings, which have pressed themselves into the background, the nuclear question demands prior attention."[56]

On December 4th, Schweitzer wrote Cousins about the latter's forthcoming trip to Europe, but warned him that he could have little leverage on German policy: "From the outside, one cannot too well influence things in Germany." He recalled how he refused to "step into the anti-atom movement with my name, in the U.S.A. The same principle holds everywhere." The fight "in one's own country has to be fought by each one."[57]

When professor Linus Pauling wrote a book, *No More War*, which included a copy of Schweitzer's Declaration, the American scientist asked Schweitzer to sign a sentence of endorsement: "By his efforts to prevent nuclear war and to bring the powerful forces of nuclear energy under international control, Professor Linus Pauling is rendering a great service to humanity." Schweitzer agreed to make those words his own, but he asked that the adjective, international, be omitted.[58]

In this same period, Bertrand Russell and Schweitzer were both asked to write an introduction to a book containing the extensive writings of Albert Einstein on world peace. Dr. Otto Nathan, one of the editors and executor of the Einstein estate, journied to Günsbach to persuade Schweitzer to write a short introduction. For some reason, the latter refused, although Russell did so.[59]

*By the end of 1958, there was a trilateral moratorium on nuclear weapons tests. Still, that year during the ten months before the moratorium went fully into effect, there was twice as much testing in one year than ever before: 111 tests, including 67 by the United States, 29 by the Soviet Union, and five by the United Kingdom. The totals from 1945 through 1958 are revealing: 196 tests for the U.S., 72 for the U.S.S.R., and 21 for the U.K., making a total of 289.*

Early in January 1959, Schweitzer continued an old cause, now with a new ally. He read that a law professor at the University of Münster published an article that nuclear weapons are against international law. He believed that "it is extremely important that this becomes known in the U.S.A." He underlined that "public opinion in the U.S.A. must realize that judicial objective is condemning nuclear weapons according to international law."[60]

In the meantime there was rising political tension over Berlin. Schweitzer felt that the crisis was a means of sidestepping the nuclear issues. In another letter to Cousins, dated March 3rd, Schweitzer commented on "how much harm the military undertakings in the Middle East and in Quemoy have done to the cause of stopping nuclear testing." He felt that they have "created an atmosphere unsuitable for negotiations." He wondered "how many people are really prepared to die because of Berlin."[61]

In August 1959, Schweitzer made his last trip to Europe. He went from Günsbach to Copenhagen and Brussels to receive awards. In December, he departed for his 14th and final sojourn to Africa, never to return to Europe. *As the year 1959 closed, the moratorium held fast. There was no nuclear weapons test by any state.* During all of 1960, Schweitzer apparently wrote only one letter to Cousins. The latter by then was beginning his quiet diplomacy for a test-ban treaty which would lead in the beginning of the Kennedy era to his playing a role as a diplomatic courier among the "improbable triumvirate"—Kennedy, Khrushchev, and Pope John XXIII.[62] In the one letter to Cousins, dated April 25th, Schweitzer volunteered that "it is necessary that the U.S.A. give up the policy which Dulles started." (John Foster Dulles died in May 1959.) Schweitzer was interested that "Stevenson begins to involve himself politically again."[63]

*During 1960, the moratorium held among the three nuclear weapons states, but on February 13th, France—and Schweitzer was a French national—detonated in the Sahara its first nuclear explosion and two others that year, all in the atmosphere. The Geneva test-ban negotiations continued, but with no agreement. France, the Soviet Union, the United Kingdom and the United States agreed to hold a Summit conference at Paris beginning May 16th that would deal primarily with the German question and disarmament. After the American U-2 plane crashed in Soviet territory on May 1st, however, Premier Khrushchev in Paris made certain demands on President Eisenhower which the latter would not accept. As a result, Khrushchev refused to participate in the Summit.*

John F. Kennedy, not Stevenson, came into the White House in 1961. There was no immediate evidence of any substantial change of American policy in disarmament, although Adlai Stevenson became U. S. Ambassador to the UN. In April, Cousins sent to Lambaréné a copy of his new book, *Dr. Schweitzer of Lambaréné,* which was an account of Cousin's 1957 visit. In an April 22 letter thanking him for the volume, Schweitzer asked, "Is it really true that Kennedy said, that, if the agreement to disarm is not reached in a few days, America would start with new and mightier tests?" Schweitzer continued: "I cannot believe it; has Kennedy really talked like that?"[64] Cousins responded only on October 2nd, telling Schweitzer of a visit he just had with Secretary of State Dean Rusk.[65] Schweitzer immediately responded, on October 10th, telling Cousins that he was "much too pessimistic!" We have to remember, Schweitzer insisted, that "we can all be wiped out by a bomb in a few minutes." He admitted that "in public I never discuss the problem of Berlin, because it is stupid. It does not merit the importance it is being given. I give my opinion only on the problem of disarmament and peace!" He added: "This is the real problem. And it is there that the people ought to raise their voices!"[66]

In an undated letter written in that same period, Schweitzer gave Cousins his opinion about the European political situation. He ended his comments by asserting that "the U.S. should have concerned itself with East Germany's independence and the peace treaty between the Soviets and East Germany, instead of letting the unsolved problem of Berlin continue, which is troubling the whole world."[67]

TESTS RESUME
*The moratorium on testing, begun in 1958, lasted for 34 months, more than midway through 1961. The Soviet Union resumed testing (mostly in the atmosphere) on August 30, 1961, but the United States gave notice in December 1959 that it no longer felt bound by the moratorium. American tests (underground) resumed on September 15th and atmospheric testing the following March. In 1961, there were ten U.S. tests, 51 Soviet tests, and two French tests. President Kennedy and Premier Khrushchev held a Summit at Vienna in June, but there were few positive by-products and soon thereafter the Berlin Wall was erected.*

In October 1961, Cousins cabled Schweitzer urging that he immediately send his objections to the resumption of testing to President Kennedy. Instead, Schweitzer cabled Cousins: "Impossible to do what you ask. Letter on the way."[68] The letter Schweitzer wrote to Cousins on October 30th recalled that he felt that he could not denounce Kennedy any more than Khrushchev. Critics would accuse him of "meddling as a stranger in trying to influence the President of the U.S." His role, as he saw it, was "to make appeals to enlighten public opinion in all countries as to the situation in which we find ourselves. To criticize the President directly would "harm the influence I might have in the U.S.A." He felt that the present situation was deplorable: "We are sinking ever more deeply into inhumanity by the resumption of tests." All this was happening because "public opinion the world over has treated lightly the dangers of nuclear radiation." Schweitzer revealed that he was "working for months on the wording of a new appeal! But it is impossible to finish it and publish it. The situation of nuclear politics never ceases to change. It is never stabilized. Therefore one cannot judge or advise. The text that I made a month ago no longer corresponds to reality. It is outdated by events. I am watching and when I think I am able to criticize and to propose, I shall speak."[69]

Six months later Schweitzer did write President Kennedy, apparently without any further coaching from Cousins. On April 20, 1962, he addressed the President as "someone who has occupied himself for a long time with the problem of atomic weapons and with the problem of peace." He took the stance that "disarmament under effective international control" is the important goal and that negotiations toward this end should not be "made questionable by unnecessary appeals for international verification of the discontinuance of testing." He declared that "only when the states agree not to carry out tests any more can promising negotiations about disarmament and peace take place." Then he took the "courage" to draw the attention of the President "to something that concerns you personally"—the hereditary effect of radioactivity on children. He closed by saying: "It was not easy for me to draw your attention to the great responsibility you hold to protect the future generations. Please, forgive me; I could not do otherwise, not only for the sake of humanity, but also out of consideration for you personally."[70]

It took the White House five weeks to respond. On June 6th, President Kennedy wrote acknowledging that "no decision I have taken in my Administration has given me more concern and sorrow than the decision to resume nuclear testing." He called it "a tragic choice; and I make it only because the alternative seemed to me to offer even greater dangers to our hopes for world peace, to unborn generations to come, and to the future of humanity." He predicted "a grave shift in the world balance of power" if only the Soviets launched a new series of tests. If the U.S.S.R. did test, and the U.S. did not, there would be a "steady increase in Soviet nuclear strength until the Communist world could be ready for a final offensive against the democracies." Kennedy ended the letter by calling his correspondent "one of the transcendent moral influences of our century."[71]

## CUBAN MISSILE CRISIS

In October 1962 came the Cuban missile crisis. This deeply troubled many people around the world, not only Soviet, American, and Cuban citizens. Among those concerned was Albert Schweitzer. On October 22nd, in the very midst of the crisis, Schweitzer wrote Cousins that "time works for those of us who wish to abolish nuclear weapons." He felt the political problems surrounding Berlin and Cuba "are, at heart, small problems." Responding to an earlier letter in which Cousins declared that "the sources of indignation over nuclear testing are drying up" and "people in the forefront of effective protest three of four years ago . . . seemed to have been numbed by events," Schweitzer suggested that the two of them "continue our struggle against nuclear arms; let us not be discouraged by the weariness of former companions in the struggle."

Then, in a postscript, Schweitzer tried to launch yet another campaign. He read that the Kennedy Administration "decided to use nuclear arms for the question of Cuba and Berlin." He called this "a new and serious decision." He felt they must "not accept this decision without protesting." Consequently, he wrote that "to start the debate, I think it might be useful for me to write an open letter to [Secretary of Defense Robert] McNamara." He enclosed the draft of such a letter—an English translation from the original German—and asked Cousins to find an American magazine that might publish it. This contained a poignant plea for "quiet, positive negotiations" because of the "great danger in which the human race finds itself."[72]

Cousins cabled Schweitzer on October 30th—after the missile crisis had reached its peak and lessened—that "turn of events in U.S. may require changes."[73] Schweitzer wrote to Cousins again immediately after receiving the cable. Despite the crisis lessening, Schweitzer persisted: "We cannot abstain from criticizing McNamara, severely and publicly"—for announcing that he would use atomic bombs. Schweitzer felt that "the idea of an atomic war to bridge the Berlin problem seems idiotic."[74] Cousins on October 30th sent a long letter to Schweitzer, explaining that McNamara belonged to "the moderate faction" within the Kennedy Administration. Much of the letter was devoted to a detailed description of the Dartmouth Conference between prominent American and Soviet citizens which occurred during the very week of the Cuban crisis.[75]

Schweitzer did not give up easily on McNamara. Writing to Cousins again, on November 11th, Schweitzer declared that "the moderate [McNamara] acted like an extremist, with unbelievable frivolity, as did President Kennedy." Schweitzer revealed that he had written to Bertrand Russell "that I am against making public approaches to Kennedy, because he is chief of state" and "a chief of state must be criticized in public only if absolutely necessary." But one "can criticize" McNamara. Since the crisis was past, however, he was "withdrawing" the letter to McNamara. Schweitzer also wrote: "You know how much I love America." Further in the letter, Schweitzer apologized: "Forgive me for being a bit strong." Then he added: "I was terrified to hear that the head of the army and the President of the U.S. deemed it useful to consider a nuclear war not only over the Cuban crisis which is their business, but as well over the Berlin crisis, which is not and which they do not understand." Schweitzer concluded his letter by suggesting that "we must create a new state of mind if the danger of a ruinous catastrophe for humanity is to be avoided." He would "work in Europe with regard to these latest developments and shall give up the idea of criticizing, as a foreigner, American personalities."[76]

On October 24th, again in the midst of the Cuban crisis, Schweitzer wrote to Bertrand Russell. He pursued the

McNamara issue. He assumed that while the negotiations were in process to stop nuclear weapons tests, "no civilized country would decide to use atomic weapons." Then he added: "Now the U.S.A. takes this step! That means the whole situation has deteriorated, has really deteriorated." He felt that Russell and himself—"we in the world"—have to "rebel against this." McNamara and Kennedy "must know that we will not yield! The matter is very serious! We have to act."[77] Russell replied quickly, on October 30th, and expressed surprise that, during the missile crisis, Khrushchev behaved "with magnanimity."[78] On November 11th, Schweitzer took up his pen and wrote Russell again. He suggested that they only attack McNamara "who is the military commander and do not mention Kennedy because he is head of state." He felt that Kennedy might "be penitent when he is spared the humiliation of a public judgement."[79]

Friends of Schweitzer and officials of the German Democratic Republic (East Germany) developed a political relationship with him, especially on nuclear issues. Schweitzer attended the University of Berlin in 1900 and was in Berlin again in 1912. Even after Berlin was split into East and West, these ties with Schweitzer were reinforced. In the early 1960s, Schweitzer accepted an honorary degree from Humboldt University in East Berlin. Walter Ulbricht, the head of the German Democratic Republic, wrote congratulating Schweitzer on his degree. Schweitzer politely replied, adding a few words about the importance of peace and reverence for life. When Ulbricht received Schweitzer's letter, he published it. This coincided with the Berlin Wall and the Berlin crisis generally. The political reaction in some West German circles was bitter against Schweitzer for seeming to declare himself in favor of the German Democratic Republic and its nuclear politics.[80]

Schweitzer received a constant stream of nuclear political information from the German Democratic Republic in the German language, some reflecting the activities of the World Peace Council and its many congresses in that period, including its Moscow Congress in 1962. Only through this source would Schweitzer have heard positive estimates of the results of these congresses, since his American correspondents were, if anything, cool toward the World Peace Council. Yet Schweitzer in his private letters appeared to regard some of these congresses favorably, especially since he was increasingly disillusioned by Washington and NATO nuclear policy. After Schweitzer died, his friends in the German Democratic Republic honored him (including the publication of five volumes of his writings), but certainly no more so than friends in many other parts of Europe and North America.

## PARTIAL TEST-BAN TREATY

*At the end of 1962, testing was conducted at a furious pace by four countries: 96 by the United States, 44 by the Soviet Union, two by the United Kingdom, and one by France, for a record total of 143 in that single year! Late in 1961 the UN General Assembly endorsed the U.S./U.S.S.R. Agreed Principles for Disarmament Negotiations and the creation of a new Eighteen-Nation Disarmament Committee. This held its first session at Geneva beginning March 1962. It established a three nation subcommittee to negotiate a test-ban treaty because the previous committee after more than 340 meetings since 1958 had been suspended.*

*President Kennedy gave a conciliatory address at American University in Washington on June 10, 1963, asserting that the United States was stopping all nuclear tests and that Premier Khrushchev and he agreed to intensify negotiations at Moscow for a test-ban treaty. The negotiations opened on July 15th and concluded on July 25th, with the initialing of the partial test-ban treaty. This prohibited tests in all environments except under the ground. The treaty was signed at Moscow on August 5th and entered into force on October 10th. By the time of the signing of the treaty, the U.S. had made 331 tests, the U.S.S.R. 185, the U.K. 23, and France eight, for a total of 547.*[81]

On July 21st, Cousins sent Schweitzer a cable informing him that the conclusion of a treaty was "now imminent." He told Schweitzer that "you are now entitled to the appreciation of all humanity."[82] There was no evidence that Schweitzer responded at the time to Cousins, but he did write directly to President Kennedy.

Schweitzer informed the President that "the treaty gives me hope that war with atomic weapons between East and West can be avoided." He called the treaty "one of the greatest events, perhaps the greatest, in the history of the world." He added, as he did when the test-ban moratorium was announced, that "when I heard of the treaty, I thought of my old friend, Dr. Einstein, with whom I joined in the fight against atomic weapons." He said that Einstein "died at Princeton in despair." Schweitzer thanked President Kennedy for his "foresight and courage." He ended by observing that the world took "the first step on the road leading to peace." Evelyn Lincoln, Kennedy's secretary, later revealed that the receipt of this letter from Schweitzer caused great excitement in the President's office and Kennedy "was extremely grateful to him for his views."[83]

Only a few months later, on December 19th, Schweitzer wrote the President's mother, Mrs. Rose Kennedy, after the President's assassination: "I do not know who else had his clearsightedness, his tenacity, and his authority and could continue his great humanitarian and political work." Schweitzer also wrote: "At present we walk in the dark again. Where are we going? Your son was one of the great personalities of the world's history. Millions of us mourn with you."[84]

On October 4th, Cousins wrote Schweitzer that he was at a luncheon at the White House to celebrate the victorious ratification of the test-ban treaty by the U.S. Senate. Schweitzer would have been "pleased, I think, to have heard the many references made to your role in bringing about a test-ban treaty." His appeal "made this a world issue for the first time." Cousins wanted to tell Schweitzer "how proud and privileged I have been to have been associated with you, however modestly, in the test-ban crusade." History will give Schweitzer his "proper share of credit for this achievement."[85]

Cousins later wrote that Schweitzer's letters "in the two years before his death reflected his hope that the test-ban treaty might carry over to control of the arms race in general." Increasingly, Cousins reported, Schweitzer's letters "seemed to reflect some fatigue."[86]

*By the end of 1963, the Soviet Union and Great Britain made no tests all that year. The United States made four atmospheric and 25 underground tests until President Kennedy announced a moratorium on June 10th and then 14 additional underground tests were made some time after the partial test-ban treaty was signed on August 5th. France, which did not sign the treaty, detonated two devices underground before the treaty was signed and one afterwards. In June the U.S. and the U.S.S.R. signed an agreement establishing a "hot line" telephone between their two capitals. In October the UN General Assembly adopted unanimously a resolution calling upon all states to refrain from introducing weapons of mass destruction into outer space. This led to the Outer Space Treaty which entered into force in 1967.*

In the meantime, Schweitzer's occasional correspondence with Bertrand Russell continued. Schweitzer became one of the nine original members of the Bertrand Russell Peace Foundation—along with Pablo Casals, Lord Boyd-Orr, Jawaharlal Nehru, and Queen Elizabeth of Belgium, with Emperor Haile Selassie of Ethiopia and President Kwame Nkrumah of Ghana later added.[87] In 1964, Russell asked Schweitzer to become a sponsor of a conference inquiring into the assassination of President Kennedy. In a letter dated August 15th, Schweitzer declined: "People have too often criticized me for concerning myself with the world's affairs, though I live in the virgin forest. You would not wish to expose me to this criticism again." In this letter he referred obliquely to the campaign by Barry Goldwater to become President of the United States and the latter's statement that he would give authority to military leaders in Europe to use tactical nuclear weapons.[88] Russell took up this cause and circulated a worldwide "appeal on the danger to the world of Goldwater's policies."[89] Yet in a letter dated October 19th, Schweitzer refused to sign the appeal—as he did other manifestos which could be construed as interfering in the domestic politics of another country. A number of leading British personalities also refused to sign this appeal.

*The year 1964 witnessed China's first detonation of an atomic device in the atmosphere. A total of 39 additional nuclear devices were detonated, all underground, by the U.S., the U.K., the U.S.S.R., and France. China did not sign the partial test-ban treaty. The Eighteen-Nation Committee continued to meet in Geneva, but the two drafts for comprehensive general*

*and complete disarmament, submitted both by the U.S.S.R. and
the U.S. in 1962, languished.* Schweitzer celebrated his ninetieth birthday on January
14, 1965. Russell and many others sent congratulatory cables.
Schweitzer replied to Russell on January 12th, two days before
his actual birthday. He reported that he spent much time
supervising the building of new additions to his hospital, but he
also occupied himself "with the great problems of peace and
atomic weapons." He wrote that it is "very fortunate" that the
United States and the Soviet Union "walk together." He concluded that "unfortunately, it does not look that I will come
once more to Europe and we will see each other again."[90]

However old and fatigued, Schweitzer was very much his
own man to the end. He did not have to lean on any ideo-
logically-dubious "secretary"—as Bertrand Russell did for
almost a decade. The relationship between Russell and Ralph
Schoenman, his secretary, was disastrous and indirectly affected Schweitzer. Russell terminated the relationship only in
1969.[91] The Schweitzer relationship with Cousins was, on the
other hand, quite different; it was creative, not exploitive.

One of Schweitzer's last letters, dated February 15th, was
to George N. Marshall, an American biographer. Schweitzer
seemed glad that "Goldwater has ceased to be a political problem." But then he wrote that "the role of the U.S.A. in Vietnam is
a great problem." He asked: "What political role is China going
to play?"[92]

In the summer of 1965, Schweitzer felt a new deterioration in the world situation, with Vietnam only one of the pressing issues. He commented to his confidants at Lambaréné:
"Perhaps I should make another world-wide radio appeal, as I
did in Oslo." He began talking to his daughter, Rhena, about
preparing another appeal: "I should make one more effort, if
only I can have the time and am not too tired."[93] This was not to
be, for on September 4, 1965, Schweitzer died at Lambaréné
and was buried along the banks of the Ogowë River.

*By the end of 1965 there were a cumulative total of 646
nuclear weapons tests by five nations: 403 by the United States,
200 by the Soviet Union, 25 by the United Kingdom, 16 by*

*France, and two by China. No appreciable progress was reported from the Eighteen-Nation Disarmament Committee at Geneva, with both France and the People's Republic of China not yet participating (and not yet signing the partial test-ban treaty). By the end of 1986 (the latest figure available) the total has more than doubled to 1,622 known nuclear explosions by six nations (including India). The number of nuclear weapons in the world stockpile is estimated to be at least 50,000.*

## Notes

1. Substantially revised from a paper delivered at a Symposium on Albert Schweitzer's Thought and Its Relationship to the Contemporary Scene, sponsored by the Albert Schweitzer Fellowship in cooperation with the Johnson Foundation, on October 21–23, 1977, at Wingspread, Racine, Wisconsin.
2. For full text, see pages 35–42 in this volume.
3. *World Armaments and Disarmament. SIPRI Yearbook 1987* (Stockholm: Stockholm International Peace Research Institute, 1987), pp. 54–55. All figures on nuclear weapons tests to 1987 given below are taken from this yearbook.
4. For full text, see pages 154–155 in this volume.
5. James Brabazon, *Albert Schweitzer: A Biography* (New York: G.P. Putnam's Sons, 1975), pp. 422, 424.
6. *Ibid.,* pp. 422–423.
7. *Ibid.,* pp. 420–421.
8. Norman Cousins, *Dr. Schweitzer of Lambaréné* (New York: Harper & Row. 1960), p. 121. Also in *Albert Schweitzer's Mission: Healing and Peace,* by Norman Cousins. (New York: W. W. Norton, 1985), p. 76.
9. Cousins, *Schweitzer of Lambaréné,* p. 186; Cousins, *Albert Schweitzer's Mission,* p. 119.
10. For full text, see pages 43–56 in this volume.
11. *The Christian Register,* December 1954, p. 17.
12. Brabazon, p. 430.
13. *To Albert Schweitzer on His Eightieth Birthday,* edited by Homer A. Jack. (Evanston, Illinois, Privately printed, 1955), pp. 37–38.
14. For abridged text, see pages 153–154 in this volume.
15. See essay by the author, "The Same First Name." *The Courier.* Summer 1986. pp. 5–9.
16. Brabazon, p. 417.
17. *Ibid.,* pp. 429–430.

18. Linus Pauling, *No More War!* (New York: Dodd, Mead. 1958) The full text, with the names of signatories, is found on pages 222-224.
19. For the text (in the original language) of all known letters in this correspondence, see "The Correspondence Between Bertrand Russell and Albert Schweitzer," by Herbert Spiegelberg, *International Studies in Philosophy,* vol. 12 (1980). For the text of selected letters, see pages 132-145 in this volume.
20. *Einstein on Peace,* edited by Otto Nathan and Heinz Norden (New York: Simon & Schuster, 1960), p. 630.
21. *Daily Herald,* April 11, 1954, p. 4.
22. For text, see pages 132-133 in this volume.
23. George Marshall and David Poling, *Schweitzer: A Biography,* (Garden City: Doubleday. 1971), pp. 243-244.
24. Cousins, *Schweitzer of Lambaréné,* pp. 165-170; Cousins, *Albert Schweitzer's Mission,* pp. 105-111.
25. Cousins, *Schweitzer of Lambaréné,* pp. 172-176; Cousins, *Albert Schweitzer's Mission,* pp. 112-115.
26. Cousins, *Schweitzer of Lambaréné,* pp. 185-186; Cousins, *Albert Schweitzer's Mission,* pp. 119-120.
27. Cousins, *Schweitzer of Lambaréné,* pp. 189-190; Cousins, *Albert Schweitzer's Mission,* p. 123. For text, see pages 146-147 in this volume.
28. Marshall and Poling, p. 285.
29. Cousins, *Albert Schweitzer's Mission,* p. 157.
30. *Ibid.,* pp. 158-159.
31. *Ibid.,* pp. 159-164.
32. *Ibid.,* pp. 164-166. For the text, see page 96 in this volume.
33. *Ibid.,* pp. 166-171.
34. Brabazon, p. 433.
35. Cousins, *Albert Schweitzer's Mission,* pp. 173-174.
36. For full text, see pages 57-67 in this volume.
37. Cousins, *Albert Schweitzer's Mission,* pp. 174-175. For the text, see pages 96-97 in this volume.
38. *Ibid.,* pp. 189-190. For abridged text, see pages 97-98 in this volume.
39. Brabazon, p. 434.
40. Cousins, *Albert Schweitzer's Mission,* pp. 197-198.
41. Letter dated August 14, 1956, in Brabazon, p. 434.
42. John Barlow Martin, *Adlai Stevenson and The World,* (New York: Anchor Books, 1978), pp. 414-415.
43. Brabazon, pp. 434-435. Full text in The Adlai E. Stevenson Papers in the Princeton University Library.

44. Brabazon, p. 442.
45. Cousins, *Albert Schweitzer's Mission*, pp. 198–199. For the text, see pages 98–99 in this volume.
46. *Ibid.*, pp. 200–201. For the text, see pages 99–100 in this volume.
47. Brabazon, p. 440. Pauling, pp. 160–178.
48. Brabazon, p. 440.
49. Cousins, *Albert Schweitzer's Mission*, pp. 208–210. For the text, see pages 101–103 in this volume.
50. For the full texts, see pages 69–91 in this volume.
51. Cousins, *Albert Schweitzer's Mission*, pp. 215–217. For the text, see pages 103–105 in this volume.
52. *Ibid.*, pp. 215–217. For the text, see pages 103–105 in this volume.
53. *Ibid.*, pp. 222–225. For the text, see pages 107–110 in this volume.
54. *Ibid.*, pp. 231–232. For the text, see pages 147–148 in this volume.
55. *Ibid.*, pp. 232–233.
56. *Ibid.*, pp. 233–236. For the text, see pages 112–114 in this volume.
57. *Ibid.*, pp. 237–238. For the text, see pages 114–116 in this volume.
58. Brabazon, p. 442.
59. From an interview with Otto Nathan by the author.
60. Cousins, *Albert Schweitzer's Mission*, p. 240.
61. *Ibid.*, pp. 241–242. For the text, see pages 116–117 in this volume.
62. Norman Cousins, *The Improbable Triumvirate*, (New York: W. W. Norton, 1978).
63. Cousins, *Albert Schweitzer's Mission*, pp. 245–246.
64. *Ibid.*, pp. 267–268.
65. *Ibid.*, pp. 268–270.
66. *Ibid.*, pp. 270–271. For the text, see pages 117–118 in this volume.
67. *Ibid.*, pp. 272–273. For the text, see pages 119–120 in this volume.
68. *Ibid.*, p. 274.
69. *Ibid.*, pp. 274–276. For the text, see pages 120–122 in this volume.
70. *Ibid.*, pp. 277–279. For the text, see pages 148–150 in this volume.
71. *Ibid.*, pp. 277–279. For the text, see pages 150–152 in this volume.

72. *Ibid.,* pp. 283–287. For the text, see pages 122–126 in this volume.
73. *Ibid.,* p. 287.
74. *Ibid.,* p. 288. For the text, see pages 126–127 in this volume.
75. *Ibid.,* pp. 289–294.
76. *Ibid.,* pp. 294–296. For the text, see pages 127–129 in this volume.
77. For the text, see pages 140–141 in this volume.
78. "Correspondence Between Bertrand Russell and Albert Schweitzer," by Spiegelberg, *International Studies in Philosophy.*
79. For the text, see pages 141–142 in this volume.
80. Brabazon, pp. 447-448.
81. *World Armaments and Disarmament. SIPRI Yearbook 1985.* (Stockholm: Stockholm International Peace Research Institute, 1985), p. 82.
82. Cousins, *Albert Schweitzer's Mission,* p. 299.
83. Marshall and Poling, p. 288.
84. Brabazon, p. 451.
85. Cousins, *Albert Schweitzer's Mission,* pp. 299–300.
86. *Ibid.,* p. 300.
87. For a description of the program and politics of the Foundation and the tax-exempt Atlantic Peace Foundation, see *The Life of Bertrand Russell,* Ronald W. Clark. (New York: Knopf, 1976), pp. 602–628.
88. Brabazon, p. 461.
89. "Correspondence Between Bertrand Russell and Albert Schweitzer," by Speigelberg, *International Studies in Philosophy.*
90. *Ibid.* For the text, see pages 142–143 in this volume.
91. "Private Memorandum Concerning Ralph Schoenman." Clark, pp. 640–651.
92. Marshall and Poling, p. 236.
93. *Ibid.,* p. 305.

*Addresses*

# 1

# Humanity and Peace

*The German Association of Book Publishers and Sellers gave an award each year of 10,000 marks to an individual promoting world peace. In 1951 Albert Schweitzer was notified of his selection and he delivered the acceptance address at Frankfurt on September 16th. The prize was presented to Schweitzer by the President of the Federal Republic of Germany, Theodor Heuss. Long-time friends, Schweitzer had performed the marriage ceremony of Heuss in 1908. Schweitzer delivered the address in the German language.*

## HUMANITY AND PEACE

I THANK the Association of German Publishers for honoring me with the award of this prize. In today's world no one should be awarded the Peace Prize for an obvious achievement; instead, those who are honored by it should consider it only as a token of encouragement for what, with modesty and simplicity, they want to do in the interest of peace. Mr. President, I thank you for the kind words you addressed to me. I think it will be in the same spirit in which you have awarded me this prize that I will now look briefly at the path to peace as it may reveal itself to us. I do this at a time when everywhere in the world people fear for peace and when the fate of mankind is in the balance. But where does this fear—this confusion in which we find ourselves—stem from? It stems from the power gained by the progress in man's knowledge and his increased technological capabilities.

The dream of those who expected the course of history to develop a superior human being has to some extent been fulfilled. Through the power we now have to control the forces of nature we once thought uncontrollable, we have in a way become supermen. But this superman suffers from one great imperfection. His common sense, unlike the power he has acquired and to which it should correspond, has not become superhuman. On the contrary, it has remained more limited than it should be. He does not possess the topmost rung of common sense which would make it unthinkable for him to use his power over the forces of nature for destructive purposes, and which could ensure that he use it for constructive and meaningful ends only. In this power lies both his greatness and his wretchedness.

Those nations, which are composed of human beings who have gone from one achievement to another until they have reached the unforseeable, have become to one another an object of fear—a fear that cannot be exorcised. Furthermore, not one of these nations can guarantee that the other will not one day face a situation when, in self-preservation, it will be forced to use this power, great as it is, just as they used it in the two world wars of the past. Because of this power we can all be condemned to inhumanity, as is the case already to a certain extent. We have become the object of fear and anxiety for one another.

The great problem we face is: how can we extricate ourselves from this wretchedness which may determine our fate? We will only find a way out when we can trust one another, when each nation is convinced that the other will not use its power for destructive purposes. But how shall we gain one another's trust? The only possible way is by having the courage to devote ourselves again to a belief in humanity. Indeed, belief in humanity is the only way one nation can assure another that it will not use its power destructively.

Belief in humanity is the highest level of thought that any philosophy can reach. It is to be found in all great thinkers of the past, whether in India, in China, or in the Middle East. It is to

be found everywhere, perhaps most clearly and more forcefully in the great Chinese thinkers Lao-Tse, Kung Tse, and
Meng-Tse. This belief in humanity is in being wherever we
come across the ideas of love and compassion. Because of his
higher awareness, it raises man above all other creatures, for in
his spiritual development he has reached such an experience
and understanding of higher things that they must now
influence all his attitudes.

The first to dare to think and express this were the
philosophers of the later school of stoicism. It was they who
conceived and gave expression to the notion of belief in
humanity, which later was brought together with the idea of
love such as is found in the Jewish prophets, in Jesus and in St.
Paul. However, these two currents of belief in humanity were
not able to come together in antiquity. They ran parallel to one
another because Christianity was taken up by its negation of
life and of this world. And neither did the later school of Stoics,
as represented by Seneca, Marcus Aurelius, or Epictetus,
although affirming life and the world, have the strength of will
to progress. These two currents were to meet only in the
Renaissance and Post-Renaissance periods with the occurrence
of the desire for progress and the affirmation of the value of
life. The humanist ethics of the later Stoics and Christianity
came together in such a way that they learned from one
another that all thought must reach its highest level with belief
in humanity, and that the love preached by Jesus does not
spring exclusively from divine revelation but is also, simultaneously, a manifestation of reason. Furthermore, in reaching
the conclusion that all superior truths are also always reasonable to the highest degree, belief in humanity has now become
a leading force in the development and defense of life and the
world, thus becoming one of the creative forces of world history. It was this belief that made the love of Jesus a positive
element in public life, and did away with the superstitions,
witch-hunts, torture, and all kinds of atrocities and misdeeds of
the past, replacing the old practices by innovations which
always surprise those who follow the process of history.

This creative force maintained its impetus for some
decades. Then, around the middle of the 19th century, it lost its

vigor and efficacy. Why did this happen? In the first place because its world view was no longer based upon a knowledge which was in accord with that of scientific research. It had to accommodate itself and survive without the support of such knowledge as then existed. The bond which had been forged in the 18th century between religion and philosophy weakened and fell apart. From this time on religion and philosophy parted and went their own separate ways. It lost its impetus because it was considered irrelevant. In fact some now believed that the course of history was to take a different direction, that its objectives no longer corresponded to the ideal of the highest spiritual and material well-being of the majority, but to something which was in itself both superior and inevitable, even if it brought misery, suffering, and sacrifice to the peoples it would affect. We saw these ideas being expressed at the end of the last century, when anti-humanism and inhumanity dared raise its head to justify things which were no longer in agreement with our sensibility and compassion.

In this way history and the situation in which we find ourselves were created. And thus arose the wretchedness resultant from the fear we have of one another and which now motivates us. Our only hope is that the spirit and belief in humanity may manifest themselves again in our lifetime.

However, let us not crave for the impossible. How shall the spirit regain the vigor it has lost? There is still hope that we may find this lost strength once again. There are still reasons to keep this hope alive and to believe that the spirit of humanity is not dead; that it lives in hiding and has managed to survive the fact that it must forego knowledge of the world. It is now conscious of the fact that it must base itself on nothing other than man's nature, gaining thus an independence and self-sufficiency which in itself is an asset and a strength. Moreover, it has now also understood that this awareness only reaches its true scope and greatest depth, and therefore its highest vitality, when it refers not only to its fellow man but encompasses everything in its domain. It needs no knowledge of life and the world, other than knowing everything which exists in life, and of recognizing that we must regard with the greatest reverence all life as being of the most precious and irreplaceable value. No natural science can withhold from humanity this most simple knowledge because it is still the most fundamental and simple fact before which each natural science must halt, recognizing that everything that exists is alive. And, therefore, in these stormy times, the idea of humanity which formed the essence of all civilizations is again in the air and it might lead us out of the misery we are faced with.

But we must keep the following in mind: if humanity is to bring us peace in the world it must also represent what is good for *all* peoples. This is more important today than at any other time because it is in our time that those nations which have hitherto had no share in the higher civilization—the underdeveloped nations—are becoming independent states in their own right. Thus the world view is totally changing.

The important question arises as to what will become of these states. Will they develop a civilization which allows them to develop a way of life most suitable to themselves and their environment; or will they persist in living in non-civilization; or, even worse, in living in an apparent civilization, which will mean the affirmation of the values of disorder in the world. And as one who lives in the still primitive world, I can tell you that this is the big problem facing the constructive creation of world history today.

As one who is also concerned with the problem of discussing civilization with those who are new to it, I can tell you that the primitive and half-primitive peoples are fit for the true civilization which embodies the spirit of humanity. We have confronted them, however, with a kind of civilization which they are not able to adopt fully. The reason lies within themselves as well as in the material things which we brought to them. We have all come to realize that they have adopted the unimportant, the subsidiary, and have overlooked the spiritual which—dare I say it aloud—is nevertheless still to be found in our civilization. We believed that the best way of familiarizing them with our civilization was first to educate them in the knowledge and technological ability which forms our culture. But they didn't make any progress because this path did not suit them. And so we now have in the world a semi-civilization, that is, a civilization in its claim but not in its achievements.

However, if the spiritual element in our civilization is a positive force it will be reflected in the societies of both primitive and half-primitive peoples, for they have something absolutely natural about them. They think about and are concerned with their own state of being, and everything relating to this self-analysis is familiar to them. And when in his self-reflection man becomes familiar with ideas which lead him simply to a higher level, then he is able to adopt without difficulty those values which raise him out of his primitivism and half-primitivism. To achieve this, all he has to do is reflect upon himself (which in all his naturalness primitive man is better able to do than we), thus raising himself to a higher level than that at which he presently stands. And knowing the spiritual situation for the still primitive world, I am encouraged to tell you the following. There is the possibility that the under-developed peoples of the world, on being confronted with a true civilization—instead of one in which the spiritual values have been eroded—will be ready to receive it, and that they will be able to make their contribution in order that peace may reign in the world.

Therefore, we trust in the spirit of humanity which already once has created the most important thing that happened in blessed history, at the beginning of the present era. And we trust in it, continuing the work which it left unfulfilled, so that it may achieve in our time what it achieved then, which is, to lead it out of something old that it can no longer tolerate, into something new that it cannot yet envisage. For the spirit of humanity is a creative spirit and therefore we trust in it not only because it remains our hope in these times, but because it is able to fulfil its historic task. As a creative spirit it has its effect from the inside. It solves all those problems which we reflect upon from the outside and which seem insoluble by working inwardly for their solution. It creates guarantees for those who are in opposition, guarantees which can be given in no other way. It is appropriate in a way that exceeds all common appropriateness. It is the highest—the most reasonable in the highest sense. And because it is so creative, like nature itself, producing a purposefulness which is its very essence, we trust in it and dare to put our fate into its hands. It is not something which we have to wait for or which we have to call for; it is something which is at our disposal. This spirit of humanity can develop in ourselves because we all possess the material out of which it strives to develop, that is, the consciousness of our highest human ability and vocation in ourselves. We have got the fuel. Now the only problem is to be willing and courageous enough to set it alight, in unison. In leading us from the absence of peace towards the way to peace between nations, we not only assign the highest task to the spirit, we also try to realize it in ourselves. For humanity cannot develop in the world if it fails to develop in every individual and if we do not dare to give it sufficient space in ourselves and in our lives. The spirit has to become a fact everywhere where there is no peace. Absence of peace not only exists between peoples but also within people themselves, and the spirit will prove its existence when it dares to attack the basis of this absence of peace between peoples. For everywhere, in each nation, justice has to replace injustice, kindness has to replace harshness, understanding must take the place of ignorance. Everywhere time has caused great wounds which have to be healed, so that the absence of peace in nations and between individuals may come to an end. This can only be done by the spirit which alone, as a creative natural force of history, can bring peace. And the creative is determined by the fact that in nature the spirit exists by itself, it produces this new thing out of the old in a purposeful, absolutely reasonable, and practical way, without our understanding it. However, the spirit which works in history doesn't exist in things themselves (this was Hegel's great mistake); it has to be created by us and made active in history through us. But when it exists it works as a mysteriously creative force in the same way as it works in nature. It creates something new in which every precious element of the old is embodied. This ensures that, as human beings in our time looking to the future, we trust in preserving old values. And in this spirit we face that which is new in our time. In our time, every manifestation of the spirit, however weak it might be, has its importance, for the fire can inflame the fuel which cannot burn by itself. Fuel for the spirit of humanism is present in the hearts of all people all over the world and we hope that one day it will burn. May these words which reflect the thoughts of millions who live, fearful for peace, in our own societies—may they, if they can reach those in other societies equally fearful for peace—may they, at a time when circumstances being as they are (it is understandable that each nation should be ready to defend itself)—may they nevertheless bring to those to whom they come, the assurance that they are spoken out of the sincere desire for and hope of peace harbored by millions, and may they be so understood.

St. Paul, the great mystic, who at the same time had such a good understanding of reality, spoke the following words as an exhortation for peace: "Above all, keep peace with all mankind." And this is not only valid for the peoples in our time. We hope that the peoples, and those who rule them, keep these words in mind and in these terrifying days, strive to ensure that the spirit be given time to help. Then only we may hope.

# 2
# The Problem of
# Peace in the World of Today

*In October 1953, the Nobel Committee of the Norwegian Parliament announced that Albert Schweitzer would be awarded the Nobel Peace Prize for 1952. (Leon Jouhaux, a French trade union leader and one of the founders of the International Labor Organization, received the Nobel Peace Prize in 1951.) Schweitzer could not travel from Africa to Europe to receive the award. In his absence, it was accepted by the French Ambassador, M. de Monicault, at Oslo on October 30, 1953.*

*Schweitzer returned to Europe in May 1954 and personally received the award on November 4th at Oslo. As part of the ceremonies, he delivered the acceptance address. He had more than a year's notice and worked on the text both in Africa and in Europe. The address delivered in the French language was widely reported and reprinted.*

---

THE PROBLEM OF PEACE IN THE WORLD OF TODAY

THE AWARD of the Nobel Peace Prize carries with it the redoubtable honor of delivering this address. In choosing for my subject "The Problem of Peace in the World of Today," I felt that I was fulfilling the wish of the founder of the Prize; for he himself had thought a great deal about the problem, as it presented itself in his lifetime, and it was with the object of furthering the cause of peace that he first founded the Nobel Prize.

I shall begin by describing the situation which faces us as a result of the two wars which we have recently lived through.

Each of these wars was followed by a period of negotiation; but the statesmen who reshaped the world during the course of these negotiations were not blessed with good fortune. They did not aim to create situations which might, in time, have resulted in an era of general prosperity; their main object was to exploit the consequences of victory and, if possible, to make them permanent. Even if they had been able to see into the future, they could not have allowed themselves to be guided by their own judgment alone; for they were obliged to reckon with the wishes of their victorious peoples, and to consider themselves as the executors of those wishes. There was no place for reflection on dignity and justice. It was all that they could do to make sure that their victorious peoples did not, in point of fact, insist on the fulfillment of their most outrageous demands. They had also, of course, to persuade the victorious Allies to offer one another such reciprocal concessions as were indispensable on occasions when their views, or their interests, did not coincide.

That the present situation is impossible, alike for victors and for vanquished, is due to our neglect of historical reality. We have not taken proper notice of history; and, in consequence, we no longer know what is just—or what is useful.

The historical problem of Europe is conditioned by the fact that in the distant past—and especially during what is called the period of the Great Invasions—invaders from the East penetrated farther and farther towards the west and the southwest, and took possession of one country after another. And sometimes a new wave of immigrants would live side by side with others who had been there for some considerable time.

In time, these immigrant groups achieved a kind of unity. New boundaries were formed, and within their limits there arose new and relatively homogeneous "nations." In western and central Europe this evolution gradually resulted in what may broadly he considered a definitive grouping. The nineteenth century saw this process completed.

In the east and south-east, on the other hand, this evolution has not progressed so far. In these regions many nationalities live side by side; but there has been no fusion comparable to that which occurred in western Europe. Each group has, to a certain extent, a claim to the ground on which it lives. Some can say that they were first on the scene; others that they are more numerous; and yet others, that they have put their land to the best use. The only practical solution would be for them to agree to live together, in the same territory, in a common national organization, according to a compromise acceptable to all. But this state of affairs would have had to be reached before the middle of the nineteenth century. For, from that period onwards, national self-consciousness became more and more intense; and the consequences were grave. Nations could no longer be guided by reason and historical truth.

In this way, the first world war had its origins in the conditions obtaining in eastern and south-eastern Europe. And in the new organization which has been created after two world wars we have the germs of a third conflict.

Any reorganization which ignores historical reality must bear within itself the seeds of war. The only solution which can be guaranteed to last is one which aims at a just and objective solution in the light of historical reality.

This reality is flouted and scorned if, when two nations have conflicting historical claims to a piece of territory, the claim of one is discounted altogether. Such claims, where European territory is concerned, can have only a relative value, in that both claimants are, in point of fact, immigrants of earlier or later date.

History is also flouted by any reorganization of Europe which fixes new frontiers without regard to the realities of economics; if, for instance, we draw a new frontier in such a way that a port is deprived of the hinterland which nature has designed for it, or if we erect a barrier between an area which is rich in raw materials and another that is able and ready to transform those materials. Such practices lead to the establishment of states which are not economically self-supporting.

The most flagrant violation of the rights of history—and, above all, of the rights of man—occurs when a people is deprived of the right to the land on which it lives and has to move elsewhere. At the end of the second world war the victorious powers decided to impose this fate upon hundreds of thousands of people, and to impose them in the cruellest conditions; in this they showed how little they understood their task, and how unfitted they were to carry out a reorganization which would be reasonably equitable and might guarantee a more prosperous future.

Our present situation is summed up in one fact: that the second world war has not been followed by any treaty of peace. The agreements which brought it to an end had the character merely of a truce; and it is because we are not able to reach any satisfactory formula for reorganization that we have to content ourselves with uncertain truces which arise from the needs of the moment and cannot be regarded as in any way permanent.

That is the situation in which we find ourselves. And now—what exactly is the problem of peace in the modern world? Its conditions are quite new—as different from those of former times as is the war which we seek to avert. Modern warfare is fought out with weapons which are incomparably more destructive than those of the past. War is, in fact, a greater evil than ever before. It was once possible to regard it as an evil to which we could resign ourselves, because it was the servant of progress—and was even essential to it. It could be argued in those days that, thanks to war, those nations which were strongest got the better of their weaker neighbors and thus determined the march of history.

It could be said, for instance, that the victory of Cyrus over the Babylonians created, in the Near East, an empire superior in civilization to that which had gone before it: and that, in its turn, the victory of Alexander the Great opened the way, from the Nile to the Indus, for Hellenic civilization. But the contrary also happened: sometimes war led to the replacement of a civilization by one which was clearly its inferior. An instance of this occurred in the seventh, and at the beginning of the eighth century, when the Arabs conquered Persia, Asia Minor, Palestine, northern Africa and Spain—countries in which the Greco-Roman civilization had previously held sway.

It is clear, however, that in former times war was as often the servant as the enemy of progress. Modern warfare, on the other hand, is such that one would hesitate a long time before claiming that it contributes to progress. It constitutes an evil—and an evil far graver than in former times.

It is worth remembering that for the generation which grew up before 1914, the enormous increase in the destructive power of modern armament was regarded as advantageous to humanity. It was argued that the outcome of any future conflict would be settled much more quickly than in previous ages, and that any such wars would therefore be very brief. This opinion was taken for granted.

It was also thought that the harm done by any future conflict would be relatively slight, since a new element of humanity was being introduced into the rules of war. This arose from the obligations established by the Geneva Convention of 1864 as a result of the efforts of the Red Cross. The nations had entered into a mutual agreement to look after each other's wounded, to ensure that prisoners of war were treated humanely, and to see that the civil populations were disturbed as little as possible. This convention did, in point of fact, have substantial results, and hundreds of thousands of men, civilians and combatants alike, have profited by it in the last ninety years. But these advantages are trifling when set beside the immeasurable harm which has been inflicted by modern methods of death and destruction. There cannot, at the present time, be any question of "humanizing" war.

Such was our faith in the brevity and relative humanity of any future war that the outbreak of war in 1914 was not taken as seriously as it should have been. It was regarded as a storm that would clear the political air—and also as something that would put an end to the armament race that was ruining every nation in Europe.

Some took the war lightly, and even welcomed it for the profits which it would bring them. Others took a loftier, more serious view: the war was to be the last of its kind, the war to end war. Many a good man went out convinced that he was fighting for a future in which war would be unknown.

In the event (and again in 1939–1945) these two theories proved completely erroneous. The struggle, and the destruction, went on for years, and were waged with the completest inhumanity. The war, unlike that of 1870, was not fought out between two isolated peoples, but between two great groups of nations, so that the majority of the human race was drawn into it, and the triumph of evil was all the greater.

Now that we know how terrible an evil war is in our time, we should neglect nothing that may prevent its recurrence. Above all, this decision must be based on ethical values: during the last two wars we were guilty of atrocious acts of inhumanity. In any future war, we shall do yet more terrible things. This must not be.

Let us be brave and look the facts in the face. Man has become a superman. He is a superman not only because he has at his command innate physical forces, but because, thanks to science and to technical advancement, he now controls the latent forces of nature and can bring them, if he wishes, into play. When quite on his own he could only kill at a distance by calling upon the personal strength which enabled him to draw his bow: and this strength he communicated to the arrow by suddenly unleashing his bow. Superman, on the other hand, has contrived to unleash something quite different: the energy released by the deflagration of a particular mixture of chemicals. This allows him to use a vastly more formidable projectile; and he can send it a great deal farther.

But this superman suffers from a fatal imperfection of mind. He has not raised himself to that superhuman level of reason which should correspond to the possession of superhuman strength. Yet it is this that he needs, if he is to put his gigantic strength to ends which are reasonable and useful, rather than destructive and murderous. For this reason the advance of science has become fatal to him, rather than advantageous.

In this respect we must remember that the first great scientific discovery—that of the strength inherent in the detonation of gunpowder—originally presented itself uniquely as a way of killing from a distance.

The conquest of the air, thanks to the internal combustion engine, was a decisive step forward for humanity. But mankind at once took advantage of it to kill and destroy from a height. This invention forced us to acknowledge something that we had previously refused to admit: that the superman is impoverished, not enriched, by the increase in his powers. If he is not to expose himself to destruction from above, he must go underground like the beasts of the field. And at the same time he must resign himself to an unprecedented abasement of cultural values.

A new stage began when it was discovered that the monstrous forces liberated by the disintegration of the atom could likewise be put to use. Soon it became clear that bombs constructed in this way were beginning to have incalculable powers of destruction; and that large-scale experiments might provoke a catastrophe that would endanger the very existence of humanity. Only now does the full horror of our position become clear to us. We can no longer evade the problem of the future of our race.

But the essential fact which must now strike home to us (and it should have struck home long ago) is that inhumanity and the superman are indissolubly linked; the one progresses in step with the other. We tolerate mass-killing in wartime— about twenty million people died in the second world war— just as we tolerate the destruction by atomic bombing of whole towns and their populations. We tolerate the use of the flame-thrower which turns living human beings into flaming torches. We learn of these things in the news, and we judge them according to whether they signify a success for the group of nations to whom we belong, or for our enemies. When we admit to ourselves that they were the direct results of an act of inhumanity, our admission is qualified by the reflection that "war is war" and there is nothing to be done about it. In so resigning ourselves, without any further resistance, we ourselves become guilty of inhumanity.

The important thing is that we should one and all acknowledge that we have been guilty of this inhumanity. The horror of that avowal must needs arouse every one of us from our torpor, and compel us to hope and to work with all our strength for the coming of an age in which war will no longer exist. These hopes, these determinations, can have one object and one only: the attainment, through a change of heart, of that state of superior reason in which we shall no longer put to evil uses the great power which is now at our disposal.

The first man who had the courage to advance purely ethical arguments against war, and to call for those superior standards to which the will-to-good can give rise, was Erasmus of Rotterdam, in his *Querella Pacis,* published in 1517. In this he describes the plight of Peace in her search for an audience.

Erasmus has had few successors. The idea that peace might be brought nearer by the affirmation of the necessity of ethics was dismissed as utopian. Kant was one of those who took this view. In his essay on "Perpetual Peace," published in 1795, and in others of his works which touch upon the subject, he asserts that peace will only come about when international law is powerful enough to appoint a court of international arbitration, and to see that its judgment is binding in all conflicts between two or more nations. Its authority, in Kant's view, would be based entirely on the ever-increasing respect with which mankind would come (for purely practical reasons) to regard the law as such. He constantly insists, when discussing the foundation of a Society of the Nations, that ethical arguments should not be advanced in its favor. It should be considered, he says, as the natural culmination of a system of law which will, in time, perfect itself. This perfection will arrive, he thinks, of its own accord. In his opinion "Nature, that great artist," will work upon mankind—very gradually, he admits, and over a very lengthy period of time—until the march of history and the sheer horror of warfare will between them persuade us all to agree to an international covenant to guarantee perpetual peace.

The first detailed plan for a League of Nations with powers of arbitration was drawn up by Sully, the friend and minister of Henry IV. It has been minutely described by the Abbé Castel de Saint-Pierre in three publications, of which the most important is entitled: "A Project for Perpetual Peace between the sovereigns of Christendom." Kant's knowledge of Sully's point of view is probably derived from an extract which Rousseau published in 1761.

Today we have a great deal of experience from which to estimate the efficacy of international institutions: the history, that is to say, of the League of Nations, and of the United Nations Organization. Such bodies can render substantial service—by offering to mediate at the outset of any dispute, by taking the initiative in the creation of international enterprises, and by other actions of this kind, as circumstances permit. One of the most important achievements of the League of Nations was the creation in 1922 of the internationally-valid Nansen passport for persons who had lost their nationality as a result of the war. The situation of such people would have been grave indeed if Nansen had not proposed the institution of this substitute passport. And what, again, would have been the lot of the displaced person, after 1945, if there had been no U.N.O.?

And yet—these two institutions have not brought about a state of general peace. Their efforts were bound to fail, because the world in which they operated was in no wise bent upon the achievement of such a peace; and they themselves, being merely juridical institutions, had no power to create a more apposite state of mind. Ethics alone has this power. Kant was mistaken when he believed that ethics was unnecessary to his pacific activities. We must follow the road upon which he did not wish to venture.

And, what is more, we no longer have the great length of time on which he was counting for the evolution of peace. The wars of our time, unlike anything he envisaged, are wars of total destruction. We must act decisively, if we are to secure peace. We must get decisive results, and get them soon. Only the spirit can do this.

But is the human spirit able to achieve those things which, in our distress, we must expect of it?

We must not underestimate its strength. Through human history this strength has made itself manifest. It is to the strength of the human mind that we owe the humanitarianism that is at the origin of all progress towards a higher way of life. When we are animated by humanitarianism we are faithful to ourselves and capable of creation. When the contrary state of mind takes hold of us, we are unfaithful to ourselves and a prey to errors of every kind.

The full potentiality of the human spirit was revealed to us during the seventeenth and eighteenth centuries. Those European nations in which it was active were dragged forth, by its agency, from the Middle Ages; superstition, witchcraft trials, the torture-chamber and many another time-honored folly and cruelty were abolished. In the place of the old the human mind created those new things which never cease to astonish those who witness them. Whatever was and is true, and personal to ourselves, in our civilization can be traced to that great manifestation of the strength of the human mind.

This strength later diminished—above all because the researches of science failed to establish any ethical foundation beneath our vastly increased knowledge of the world. Man no longer knew quite in which direction he should progress. His ideals grew less lofty. But now today we must once again abandon ourselves—if we do not wish to go to our destruction—to that pristine strength of the human spirit. It must bring about a new miracle—one comparable to that which lifted the nations of Europe clear of the Middle Ages, but even greater in scope.

The human spirit is not dead: it lives on in secret. Compelled to live on without that knowledge of the world which would correspond to its ethical character, it has contrived to do so. It has understood that it must base itself on nothing but the essential character of man. Now independent of all other knowledge, it is the stronger for that independence. It has come to believe that compassion, in which all ethics must take root, can only attain its full breadth and depth if it embraces all living creatures and does not limit itself to mankind. Ancient ethics had not this depth, this strength of conviction; but beside it there now stands a new ethic—that of respect for life, whose validity is more and more widely acknowledged.

Once again we are venturing to address ourselves to the whole nature of man, to his faculties of feeling and thought, and to urge him to know himself and to be faithful to that knowledge. Once again we seek to place our trust in the deepest qualities of his nature. Recent experience confirms that we are right in doing so.

In 1950 there appeared a book called *Documents of Humanity*. It was published by certain professors at Göttingen University who had been caught up in the horrible mass expulsion of East Germans in 1945. It is a book in which refugees describe, quite simply, how they were helped in their misfortunes by people who belonged to enemy nations and should therefore have been animated by hatred towards them. Rarely have I been so deeply affected by a book. Those who have lost faith in humanity should read it; it may change their minds.

Whether we secure a lasting peace will depend upon the direction taken by individuals—and, therefore, by the nations whom those individuals collectively compose. This is even more true today than it was in the past. Erasmus, Sully, the Abbé Castel de Saint-Pierre and those others who, in their time, were preoccupied with the problem of peace had not to deal with whole peoples, but with princes. What they had in mind was the creation of a supra-national authority with powers of arbitration in cases where one prince fell out with another. Kant, in his *Perpetual Peace,* was the first to envisage a period in which peoples would govern themselves and would therefore have to be concerned, as sovereign bodies, with the problem of peace. He considered this development as a step forward. In his opinion, peoples would be more likely than princes to keep the peace, because it is they who have to endure all the misfortunes of war.

Today our rulers are expected to consider themselves as the executors of the people's will. But Kant's faith in the people's innate love of peace has not been vindicated. The "will of the people" is the will of a multitude; and, as such, it has not escaped the dangers of instability. Passions have turned it aside from the path of true reason; it has proved lacking in that feeling for responsibility which is vital to it. The worst kind of nationalism has manifested itself during the two wars and is at this moment the greatest obstacle to international understanding.

This nationalism can only be overthrown by the rebirth, in all mankind, of a humanitarian ideal; attachment to one's fatherland would then become natural, healthful, and ideal in character.

Nationalism of the evil variety is virulent also in many distant countries—above all in those which formerly were subject to the white nations, and have not long recovered their independence. They are running the risk of making this naive nationalism their sole ideal. Consequently there are many regions whose long history of peace is now in jeopardy.

These peoples, too, will only be able to rise above their simple-minded nationalism if they espouse some humanitarian ideal. But how will the change come about? Only when the human spirit grows powerful within us and guides us back to a civilization based on the humanitarian ideal; only then will it act, through our intermediacy, upon those other peoples. All men, even the half-civilized, even the savages, are endowed with the faculty of compassion, and for this reason can develop the humanitarian spirit. There is inflammable matter within them: let there come a spark, and it will burst into flame.

History shows several instances of peoples which, having reached a certain level of civilization, give voice to the conviction that the reign of peace will eventually come to pass. In Palestine this belief was first propounded by the prophet Amos, in the eighth century B.C., and it lived on in the Jewish and Christian religions in the form of the hoped-for Kingdom of God. It forms one element in the teaching of the great Chinese thinkers: Confucius and Lao-Tse in the sixth century B.C., Mi-Tse in the fifth century, and Meng-Tse in the fourth. It recurs in Tolstoy, and in other European thinkers. It has been discounted as "utopian"; but the situation today is such that it must in one way or another become reality if humanity is not to perish.

I am well aware that there is nothing essentially new in what I have been saying about the problem of peace. I am profoundly convinced that the solution is this: we should reject war for ethical reasons—because, that is to say, it makes us guilty of the crime of inhumanity. Erasmus of Rotterdam, and several others since his day, have proclaimed this as the truth to which all should rally.

The only originality which I claim for myself is that not only do I affirm this as true, but I am convinced, intellectually convinced, that the human spirit in our time is capable of creating a new attitude of mind: an attitude based upon ethics. This conviction persuades me to affirm that truth anew, in the hope that my testimony may perhaps prevent its being set aside as a well-meaning form of words. People may say that it is "inapplicable to reality"; but more than one truth has long remained dormant and ineffective for no other reason than that nobody had imagined that it could ever have any application to reality.

Only to the extent in which the peoples of the world foster within themselves the ideal of peace will those institutions whose object is the preservation of that peace be able to function as we expect, and hope, that they will.

Today, once again, we live in a period that is marked by the absence of peace; today, once again, nations feel themselves menaced by other nations; today, once again, we must concede to each the right to defend himself with the terrible weapons which are now at our disposal.

Such are the circumstances in which we await the first sign of that manifestation of the spirit in which we must place our trust. This sign can take only one form: the beginnings of an attempt by every nation to repair, as far as possible, the wrongs which each inflicted upon the other during the last war. Hundreds of thousands of prisoners and deportees are still waiting to go back to their homes; others, unjustly condemned by a foreign power, still await their acquittal; these and many another injustice have yet to be set right.

In the name of all those who are striving for peace, I venture to ask the people of all nations to take the first step upon this new road. None of them will sacrifice, in so doing, an iota of the power which he needs for his own defense.

If, in this way, we can begin to liquidate the war which has just finished, a new confidence may start to arise between nations. Confidence is, in every enterprise, the supreme capital, without which nothing of real use can be done. It creates, in every sphere of life, the conditions of fruitful development. Once this atmosphere of trust is created we can turn to an equitable settlement of the problems which two great wars have left behind them.

I believe that I have here given voice to the thoughts and hopes of millions of human beings in our part of the world who live in fear of a future war. May my words be understood in their true sense, if they happen to reach those on the far side of the barrier who are haunted by this same fear.

May those who have in their hands the fate of the nations take care to avoid whatever may worsen our situation and make it more dangerous. And may they take to heart the words of the Apostle Paul: "If it be possible, as much as lieth in you, live peaceably with all men." His words are valid not only for individuals but for whole nations as well. May the nations, in their efforts to keep peace in being, go to the farthest limits of possibility so that the spirit of man shall be given time to develop and grow strong—and time to act.

# 3

# A Declaration of Conscience

*A number of persons urged Albert Schweitzer, especially after he received the Nobel Peace Prize in 1953, to speak out against nuclear weapons tests then being conducted by the Soviet Union, the United Kingdom, and the United States. By 1954 there was evidence that the tests were causing damage to human beings through radioactive fallout.*

*American editor Norman Cousins visited Schweitzer at Lambaréné in January 1957 in the hope that Schweitzer might publicly oppose nuclear testing. Reluctantly, Schweitzer agreed to do so. Schweitzer then persuaded the Norwegian Nobel Committee in effect to sponsor a broadcast over Radio Oslo. Gunnar Jahn, head of the Nobel Committee, read Schweitzer's speech in the Norwegian language (as translated from the original German). It was then broadcast in other European languages on short wave and eventually throughout the world. The world press carried excerpts. The Declaration was soon printed in many languages.*

A DECLARATION OF CONSCIENCE

SINCE March 1, 1954 hydrogen bombs have been tested by the United States at the Pacific island of Bikini in the Marshall group and by Soviet Russia in Siberia. We know that testing of atomic weapons is something quite different from testing of non-atomic ones. Earlier, when a new type of giant gun had been tested, the matter ended with the detonation. After the explosion of a hydrogen bomb that is not the case. Something remains in the air, namely, an incalculable number of radioactive particles emitting radioactive rays. This was also the case with the uranium bombs dropped on Nagasaki and Hiroshima and those which were subsequently tested. However, because these bombs were of smaller size and less effectiveness compared with the hydrogen bombs, not much attention was given to this fact.

Since radioactive rays of sufficient amount and strength have harmful effects on the human body, it must be considered whether the radiation resulting from the hydrogen explosions that have already taken place represents a danger which would increase with new explosions.

In the course of the three-and-a-half years that have passed since then [the test explosions of the early hydrogen bombs] representatives of the physical and medical sciences have been studying the problem. Observations on the distribution, origin, and nature of radiation have been made. The processes through which the human body is harmfully affected have been analyzed. The material collected, although far from complete, allows us to draw the conclusion that radiation resulting from the explosions which have already taken place represents a danger to the human race—a danger not to be underrated—and that further explosions of atomic bombs will increase this danger to an alarming extent.

This conclusion has repeatedly been expressed, especially during the last few months. However, it has not, strange to say, influenced public opinion to the extent that one might have expected. Individuals and peoples have not been aroused to give to this danger the attention which it unfortunately deserves. It must be demonstrated and made clear to them.

I raise my voice, together with those of others who have lately felt it their duty to act, through speaking and writing, in warning of the danger. My age and the generous understanding so many people have shown of my work permit me to hope that my appeal may contribute to the preparing of the way for the insights so urgently needed.

My thanks go to the radio station in Oslo, the city of the Nobel Peace Prize, for making it possible for that which I feel I have to say to reach far-off places.

What is radioactivity?

Radioactivity consists of rays differing from those of light in being invisible and in being able to pass not only through glass but also through thin metal discs and through layers of cell tissue in the human and animal bodies. Rays of this kind were first discovered in 1895 by the physicist Wilhelm Roentgen of Munich, and were named after him.

In 1896 the French physicist Henri Becquerel demonstrated that rays of this kind occur in nature. They are emitted from uranium, an element known since 1786.

In 1898 Pierre Curie and his wife discovered in the mineral pitchblende, a uranium ore, the strongly radioactive element radium.

The joy caused by the fact that such rays were at the disposal of humanity was at first unmixed. It appeared that they influence the relatively rapidly growing and relatively rapidly decaying cells of malignant tumors and sarcomas. If exposed to these rays repeatedly for a longer period, some of the terrible neoplasms can be destroyed.

After a time it was found, however, that the destruction of cancer cells does not always mean the cure of cancer and also, that the normal cells of the body may be seriously damaged if long exposed to radioactivity.

When Mme. Curie, after having handled uranium ore for four years, finally held the first gram of radium in her hand there appeared abrasions in the skin which no treatment could cure. With the years she grew steadily sicker from a disease caused by radioactive rays which damaged her bone marrow and through this her blood. In 1934 death put an end to her suffering.

Even so, for many years we were not aware of the grave risks involved in x-rays to those constantly exposed to them. Through operating x-ray apparatus thousands of doctors and nurses have incurred incurable diseases.

Radioactive rays are material things. Through them the radioactive element constantly and forcefully emits tiny particles of itself. There are three kinds. They are named after the three first letters of the Greek alphabet, *alpha, beta, gamma.* The gamma rays are the hardest ones and have the strongest effect.

The reason why elements emit radioactive rays is that they are in a continuous state of decaying. The radioactivity is the energy liberated little by little. There are other elements besides uranium and radium which are radioactive. To the radiation from the elements in the earth is added some radiation from space. Fortunately, the air mass 400 kilometers high that surrounds our earth protects us against this radiation. Only a very small fraction of it reaches us.

We are, then, constantly being exposed to radioactive radiation coming from the earth and from space. It is so weak, however, that it does not hurt us. Stronger sources of radiation, as for instance x-ray machines and exposed radium, have, as we know, harmful effects if one is exposed to them for some time.

The radioactive rays are, as I said, invisible. How can we tell that they are there and how strong they are?

Thanks to the German physicist Hans Geiger, who died in 1945 as a victim to x-rays, we have an instrument which makes that possible. This instrument is called the Geiger counter; it consists of a metal tube containing rarefied air. In it are two metal electrodes between which there is a high potential. Radioactive rays from the outside affect the tube and release a discharge between the two electrodes. The stronger the radiation the quicker the discharges follow one another. A small device connected to the tube makes the discharge audible. The Geiger counter performs a veritable drum-roll when the discharges are strong.

There are two kinds of atom bomb—uranium bombs and hydrogen bombs. The effect of a uranium bomb is due to a process which liberates energy through the fission of uranium. In the hydrogen bomb the liberation of energy is the result of the transformation of hydrogen into helium.

It is interesting to note that this latter process is similar to that which takes place in the center of the sun, supplying it with the self-renewing energy which it emits in the form of light and heat.

In principle, the effect of both bombs is the same. But according to various estimates the effect of one of the latest hydrogen bombs is 2000 times stronger than the one which was dropped on Hiroshima. To these two bombs has recently been added the cobalt bomb, a kind of super atom bomb. It is a hydrogen bomb surrounded by a layer of cobalt. The effect of this bomb is estimated to be many times stronger than that of hydrogen bombs that have been made so far.

The explosion of an atom bomb creates an unconceivably large number of exceedingly small particles of radioactive elements which decay like uranium or radium. Some of these particles decay very quickly, others more slowly, and some of them extraordinarily slowly. The strongest of these elements cease to exist only ten seconds after the detonation of the bomb. But in this short time they may have killed a great number of people in a circumference of several miles.

What remains are the less powerful elements. In our time it is with these we have to contend. It is of the danger arising from the radioactive rays emitted by these elements that we must be aware.

Of these elements some exist for hours, some for weeks, or months, or years, or millions of years, undergoing continuous decay. They float in the higher strata of air as clouds of radioactive dust. The heavy particles fall down first. The lighter ones will stay in the air for a longer time or come down with rain or snow. How long it will take before everything carried up in the air by the explosions which have taken place till now has disappeared no one can say with any certainty. According to some estimates, this will be the case not earlier than thirty or forty years from now.

When I was a boy I witnessed how dust hurled into the air from the explosion in 1883 of the island Krakatoa in the Sunda group was noticeable for two years afterwards to such an extent that the sunsets were given extraordinary splendor by it.

What we can state with certainty, however, is that the radioactive clouds will constantly be carried by the winds around the globe and that some of the dust, by its own weight, or by being brought down by rain, snow, mist, and dew, little by little, will fall down on the hard surface of the earth, into the rivers, and into the oceans.

Of what nature are these radioactive elements, particles of which were carried up in the air by the explosion of atom bombs and which are now falling down again?

They are strange variants of the usual nonradioactive elements. They have the same chemical properties, but a different atomic weight. The same element can occur in several radioactive variants. Besides Iodine 131, which lives for sixteen days only, we have Iodine 129, which lives for 200,000,000 years.

Dangerous elements of this kind are: Phosphorus 32, Calcium 45, Iodine 131, Iron 55, Bismuth 210, Plutonium 239, Cerium 144, Strontium 89, Cesium 137. If the hydrogen bomb is covered by cobalt, Cobalt 60 must be added to the list.

Particularly dangerous are the elements combining long life with a relatively strong efficient radiation. Among them Strontium 90 takes the first place. It is present in very large amounts in the radioactive dust. Cobalt 60 must also be mentioned as particularly dangerous.

The radioactivity in the air, increased through these elements, will not harm us from the outside, not being strong enough to penetrate the skin. It is another matter with respiration, through which radioactive elements can enter our bodies. But the danger which has to be stressed above all the others is the one which arises from our drinking radioactive water and our eating radioactive food as a consequence of the increased radioactivity in the air.

Following the explosions of Bikini and Siberia, rain falling over Japan has, from time to time, been so radioactive that the water from it cannot be drunk. Not only that: Reports of radioactive rainfall are coming from all parts of the world where analyses have recently been made. In several places the water has proved to be so radioactive that it was unfit for drinking.

Well-water becomes radioactive to any considerable extent only after longer periods of heavy rainfall.

Wherever radioactive rainwater is found the soil is also radioactive—and in a higher degree. The soil is made radioactive not only by the downpour, but also from radioactive dust falling on it. And with the soil the vegetation will also have become radioactive. The radioactive elements deposited in the soil pass into the plants, where they are stored. This is of importance, for as a result of this process it may be the case that we are threatened by a considerable amount of radioactive elements.

The radioactive elements in grass, when eaten by animals whose meat is used for food, will be absorbed and stored in our bodies.

In the case of cows grazing on contaminated soil, the absorption is effected when we drink their milk. In that way small children run an especially dangerous risk of absorbing radioactive elements.

When we eat contaminated cheese and fruits the radioactive elements stored in them are transferred to us.

What this storing of radioactive material implies is clearly demonstrated by the observations made when, on one occasion, the radioactivity of the Columbia River in North America was analyzed. The radioactivity was caused by the atomic plants at Hanford, which produce plutonium for atomic bombs and which empty their waste water into the river. The radioactivity of the river water was insignificant. But the radioactivity of the river plankton was 2000 times higher, that of the ducks eating plankton 40,000 times higher, that of the fish 15,000 times higher. In young swallows fed on insects caught by their parents in the river the radioactivity was 500,000 times higher, and in the egg yolks of water birds more than 1,000,000 times higher.

From official and unofficial sources we have been assured, time and time again, that the increase in radioactivity of the air does not exceed the amount which the human body can tolerate without any harmful effects. This is just evading the issue. Even if we are not directly affected by the radioactive material in the air, we are indirectly affected through that which has fallen down, is falling down, and will fall down. We are absorbing this through radioactive drinking water and through animal and vegetable foodstuffs, to the same extent as radioactive elements are stored in the vegetation of the region in which we live. Unfortunately for us, nature hoards what is falling down from the air.

None of the radioactivity of the air, created by the explosion of atom bombs, is so unimportant that it may not, in the long run, become a danger to us through increasing the amount of radioactivity stored in our bodies.

What we absorb of radioactivity is not spread evenly in all cellular tissue. It is deposited in certain parts of our body, particularly in the bone tissue and also in the spleen and in the liver. From those sources the organs which are especially sensitive to it are exposed to radiation. What the radiation lacks in strength is compensated for by time. It works day and night without interruption.

How does radiation affect the cells of an organ?

Through being ionized, that is to say, electrically charged. This change means that the chemical processes which make it possible for the cells to do their job in our body no longer function as they should. They are no longer able to perform the tasks which are of vital importance to us. We must also bear in mind that a great number of the cells of an organ may degenerate or die as a result of radiation.

What are the diseases caused by internal radiation? The same diseases that are known to be caused by external radiation.

They are mainly serious blood diseases. The cells of the red bone marrow, where the red and white blood corpuscles are formed, are very sensitive to radioactive rays. It is these corpuscles, found in great numbers in the blood, which make it possible for it to play such an important part. If the cells in the bone marrow are damaged by radiation they will produce too few or abnormal, degenerating blood corpuscles. Both cases lead to blood diseases and, frequently, to death. These were the diseases that killed the victims of x-rays and radium rays.

It was one of these diseases that attacked the Japanese fisherman who were surprised in their vessel by radioactive ashes falling down 240 miles from Bikini after the explosion of an hydrogen bomb. With one exception, they were all saved, being strong and relatively mildly affected, through continuous blood transfusions.

In the cases cited the radiation came from the outside. It is unfortunately very probable that internal radiation affecting the bone marrow and lasting for years will have the same effect, particularly since the radiation goes from the bone tissue to the bone marrow. As I have said, the radioactive elements are by preference stored in the bone tissue.

Not our own health only is threatened by internal radiation, but also that of our descendants. The fact is that the cells of the reproductive organs are particularly vulnerable to radiation which in this case attacks the nucleus to such an extent that it can be seen in the microscope.

To the profound damage of these cells corresponds a profound damage to our descendants.

It consists in stillbirths and in the births of babies with mental or physical defects.

In this context also, we can point to the effects of radiation coming from the outside.

It is a fact—even if the statistical material being published in the press needs checking—that in Nagasaki, during the years following the dropping of the atom bomb, an exceptionally high occurence of stillbirths and of deformed children was observed.

In order to establish the effect of radioactive radiation on posterity, comparative studies have been made between the descendants of doctors who have been using X-ray apparatus over a period of years and descendants of doctors who have not. The material of this study comprises about 3,000 doctors in each group. A noticeable difference was found. Among the descendants of radiologists a percentage of stillbirths of 1.403 was found, while the percentage among the nonradiologists were 1.222.

In the first group 6.01 per cent of the children had congenital defects, while only 4.82 per cent in the second.

The number of healthy chidren in the first group was 80.42 per cent; the number in the other was significantly higher, viz. 83.23 per cent.

It must be remembered that even the weakest of internal radiation can have harmful effects on our descendants.

The total effect of the damage done to descendants of ancestors who have been exposed to radioactive rays will not, in accordance with the laws of genetics, be apparent in the generations coming immediately after us. The full effects will appear only 100 or 200 years later.

As the matter stands we cannot at present cite cases of serious damage done by internal radiation. To the extent that such radiation exists it is not sufficiently strong and has not lasted long enough to have caused the damage in question. We can only conclude from the harmful effects known to be caused by external radiation to those we must expect in the future from internal radiation.

If the effect of the latter is not as strong as that of the former, it may become so, through working little by little and without interruption. The final result will be the same in both cases.

Their effects add up.

We must also remember that internal radiation, in contrast to that coming from the outside, does not have to penetrate layers of skin, tissues, and muscles to hit the organs. It works at close range and without any weakening of its force.

When we realize under what conditions the internal radiation is working, we cease to underrate it. Even if it is true that, when speaking of the dangers of internal radiation, we can point to no actual case, can only express our fear, that fear is so solidly founded on facts that it attains the weight of reality in determining our attitude. We are forced to regard every increase in the existing danger through further creation of radioactive elements by atom bomb explosions as a catastrophe for the human race, a catastrophe that must be prevented.

There can be no question of doing anything else, if only for the reason that we cannot take the responsibility for the consequences it might have for our descendants.

They are threatened by the greatest and most terrible danger.

That radioactive elements created by us are found in nature is an astounding event in the history of the earth and the human race. To fail to consider its importance and its consequences would be a folly for which humanity would have to pay a terrible price. We are committing a folly in thoughtlessness. It must not happen that we do not pull ourselves together before it is too late. We must muster the insight, the seriousness, and the courage to leave folly and to face reality.

This is at bottom what the statesmen of the nations producing atomic bombs are thinking, too. Through the reports they are receiving they are sufficiently informed to form their own judgments, and we must also assume that they are alive to their responsibility.

At any rate, America and Soviet Russia and Britain are telling one another again and again that they want nothing more than to reach an agreement to end the testing of atomic weapons. At the same time, however, they declare that they cannot stop the tests as long as there is no such agreement.

Why do they not come to an agreement? The real reason is that in their own countries there is no public opinion asking for it. Nor is there any such public opinion in other countries, with the exception of Japan. This opinion has been forced upon the Japanese people because, little by little, they will be hit in a most terrible way by the evil consequences of all the tests.

An agreement of this kind presupposes reliability and trust. There must be guarantees preventing the agreement from being signed by anyone intending to win important tactical advantages foreseen only by him.

Public opinion in all nations concerned must inspire and accept the agreement.

When public opinion has been created in the countries concerned and among all nations, an opinion informed of the dangers involved in going on with the tests and led by the reason which this information imposes, then the statesmen may reach an agreement to stop the experiments.

A public opinion of this kind stands in no need of plebiscites or of forming of committees to express itself. It works through just being there.

The end of further experiments with atom bombs would be like the early sunrays of hope which suffering humanity is longing for.

# 4

# Peace or Atomic War?

*T*he concept of broadcasting "A Declaration of Conscience" was so successful that Albert Schweitzer by the autumn of 1957 began to conceive of a second radio effort. The Norwegian Nobel Committee and Radio Oslo were again willing. Over the year he accumulated much more material on nuclear politics. This reflected much wider issues than only nuclear weapons tests. Indeed, the material was abundant enough that there was not one broadcast, but three—on April 28, 29, and 30, 1958. The text was again in Norwegian—translated from the German—for the home service of Radio Oslo. It was also widely broadcast in other languages in Europe, Africa, Asia, Australia, and North and South America.

The manuscript was entitled, "Peace or Atomic War?" It was originally divided into two parts, with the second then also divided. The titles of what became three broadcasts were "The Renunciation of Nuclear Tests," "The Danger of an Atomic War," and "Negotiations at the Highest Level." Schweitzer in a letter to Norman Cousins a few weeks later wrote: "I want it to be published in a paperback booklet in many countries. I ask you to find a good courageous publisher for it in the U.S.A. . . . You can believe me that the appeals will have their best effect only after being spread to the people, in an inexpensive edition. Magazines must be allowed to reprint them at low costs . . . It has to be quite a simple, cheap edition. The sooner it is published the better."

The three broadcasts were published by Schweitzer's regular publishers, including Henry Holt in New York City,

*Adam and Charles Black in London, and by others around the world.*

---

## THE RENUNCIATION OF NUCLEAR TESTS

IN April of last year I raised my voice, together with others, to draw attention to the great danger of radioactive poisoning of the air and the earth, following tests with atom (uranium) bombs and hydrogen bombs. With others I appealed to the nuclear powers to come to an agreement to stop the tests as soon as possible, while declaring their genuine desire to renounce the use of atomic weapons.

At the time there was reasonable hope that this step would be taken. It was not to be. The negotiations in London last summer, led by Mr. Harold Stassen of the United States, achieved nothing. The conference arranged by the United Nations in the autumn of last year suffered the same fate through the withdrawal of the Soviet Union from the discussions.

The Soviet Union has recently made a disarmament proposal, on the basis of which discussions are apparently being planned. As a first step the plan presupposes that nuclear tests should cease immediately.

What chance has this condition of being fulfilled?

It might be thought that it would be easy for all those involved to reach agreement on this point. None of them would have to sacrifice any of the atomic weapons in their possession, and the handicap of not being able to try out new ones would be the same for all.

Even so, the proposal is difficult for the United States and Britain to accept. They spoke against it when the matter was discussed in the spring of 1957. Since then ceaseless propaganda has been directed against the view that the radiation following nuclear tests is so dangerous that it is necessary to stop them. The American and European Press is constantly receiving abundant propaganda material supplied by government atomic commissions and scientists, who feel called upon to support this view.

From a statement issued by the subcommittee of the American Atomic Energy Commission I quote the following phrases: "Within the framework of scientific and military requirements, it is advisable that nuclear tests are limited to a minimum. The necessary steps should be taken to correct the present confusion of the general public. The present and potential effects on heredity from the gradual increase in radioactivity of the air are kept within tolerable limits. The possibility of a harmful effect which people believe to be beyond control, has a strong emotional effect. The continuation of nuclear tests is necessary and justified in the interests of national security."

What is meant by "the confusion of the public" is the fact that people are becoming increasingly aware of dangers resulting from nuclear tests.

The meaning of the obscure statement that the "effects on heredity of the increase in radioactivity of the air are kept within tolerable limits" is that the number of children who will be born deformed, as a result of the harm done to the sexual cells, supposedly will not be large enough to justify the stopping of the tests.

The view of the scientists who feel called upon to reduce the danger of radioactivity to what they believe to be its right proportions is expressed by a Central European scientist who concluded a speech on this subject with the following bold, prophetic words: "If the tests are carried on with the same frequency as in the last few years, the radioactive poisoning will be four times stronger in 1983 than at present, and about six times stronger around the year 2010. Even that strength would be small compared with natural radiation. It can be stated categorically that the risk for mankind involved in nuclear tests is small. That is not to say that there is no risk. In this context I should like to quote the words of the American physicist and member of the Atomic Commission, Professor Dr. Libby: 'The risk of radioactive poisoning must be balanced against the risk to which the entire free world would be exposed if nuclear tests were abandoned before a safe international disarmament agreement has been brought about. The tests are necessary if the United States are not to be left behind in the development of nuclear weapons.' "

During the continued reassurance campaign a very prominent American nuclear physicist went to the length of declaring that the total number of luminous watch-dials in the world represents a greater danger than the radioactive fall-out of nuclear tests up till now.

The reassurance propaganda expects much from the glad tidings that science has succeeded in making the prototype of a hydrogen bomb producing far less of dangerous radioactive materials than the usual ones. The new bomb is called "the clean hydrogen bomb." The old type must from now on be content to be called the dirty bomb.

The clean hydrogen bomb differs from the other in having a jacket made of a material which does not, like uranium 238, release immense quantities of radioactive elements at the enormous explosive temperature. That is why it is less harmful as regards radioactivity. It is also, however, less powerful.

The new, highly praised hydrogen bomb is—let it be said in passing—only relatively clean. Its trigger is a uranium bomb made of the fissionable uranium 235—an atomic bomb as powerful as the one dropped over Hiroshima. This bomb, when detonated, also produces radioactivity, as do the neutrons released in great numbers at the explosion.

In an American newspaper at the beginning of this year, Edward Teller, the father of the dirty hydrogen bomb, sang a hymn of praise to the idyllic nuclear war to be waged with completely clean hydrogen bombs. He insists on a continuation of the tests, to perfect this ideal bomb: "Further tests will put us in a position to fight our opponents' war machine, while sparing the innocent bystanders. Clean weapons of this kind will reduce unnecessary casualties in a future war."

Of course, neither the United States nor the Soviet Union is thinking of producing this less effective bomb for use in a possible war. The American War Department has quite recently declared that the irradiation of whole areas has become a new offensive weapon.

The clean hydrogen bomb is intended for window-dressing only, not for use. The bomb is to encourage people to believe that future nuclear tests will be followed by less and less radiation, and that there is no argument against the continuation of the tests.

Those who think that the danger created by nuclear tests is small mainly take air-radiation into consideration, persuading themselves that the danger limit has not yet been reached. The results of their arithmetic are, however, not so reliable as they would like to believe. Through the years the toleration limit for radiation has had to be reduced several times. In 1934 it was 100 radiation units per year. At present the limit is officially put at 5. In many countries it is even lower. Dr. Lauriston Taylor (U.S.A.), who is regarded as an authority on protection against radiation, holds with others that it is an open question whether there is anything called a harmless amount of radiation. He thinks that we can only speak of an amount of radiation which we regard as tolerable.

We are constantly being told about "a permissible amount of radiation." Who permitted it? Who has any right to permit it?

When speaking about the risk of radiation we must take into consideration not only the radiation coming from the outside, but also that coming from radioactive elements in our body.

What is the source of this radioactivity? The radioactive elements released in the air by nuclear tests do not stay there permanently. In the form of radioactive rain and radioactive snow they fall down on the earth. They enter the plants through leaves and roots and stay there. We absorb them through the plants by drinking milk from the cows or by eating the meat of animals which have fed on them. Radioactive rain infects our drinking water.

The most powerful radioactive poisoning occurs in the areas between the Northern latitudes 10 degrees and 60 degrees, because of the numerous nuclear tests conducted mainly in these latitudes by the Soviet Union and the United States.

The radioactive elements absorbed over the years by our body are not evenly distributed in the cellular tissue, but are deposited and accumulated at certain points. From these points the internal radiation takes place, causing injuries to particularly vulnerable organs. What this kind of radiation lacks in strength is made up for by its persistence, working as it does, day and night for years.

It is a well-known fact that one of the most widespread and dangerous elements absorbed by us is Strontium 90. It is stored in the bones and emits from there its rays into cells of red bone marrow, where the red and white corpuscles are made. Blood diseases—fatal in most cases—are the result. The cells of the reproductive organs are particularly sensitive to this element. Even relatively weak radiation may lead to fatal consequences.

The most sinister aspect of both internal and external radiation is that years may pass before the evil consequences appear. Indeed, they make themselves felt, not in the first or second generation, but in the following ones. Generation after generation, for centuries to come, will witness the birth of an ever-increasing number of children with mental and physical defects.

It is not for the physicist, choosing to take into account only the radiation from the air, to say the decisive word on the dangers of nuclear tests. That right belongs to the biologists and physicians who have studied internal as well as external radiation, and those physicists who pay attention to the facts established by the biologists and physicians.

The declaration signed by 9,235 scientists of all nations, handed to the Secretary-General of the United Nations by the well-known American scientist, Dr. Linus Pauling, on 13th January 1958, gave the reassurance propaganda its death-blow. The scientists declared that the radioactivity gradually created by nuclear tests represents a greater danger for all parts of the world, particularly serious because its consequence will be an increasing number of deformed children in the future. For this reason they demanded an international agreement putting an end to the nuclear tests.

Propaganda for the continuation of nuclear tests can no longer maintain that the scientists do not agree on the question of the danger of radiation, and that one must, therefore, await the decision of international bodies and abstain from alarming the public by saying that radiation represents an actual danger, growing more serious every day.

This propaganda will continue to set the tone in certain newspapers. But beside it the truth about the danger of nuclear tests marches imperturbably along, influencing an ever-increasing section of public opinion. In the long run, even the most efficiently organized propaganda can do nothing against the truth.

One incomprehensible aspect of the propaganda for the continuation of nuclear tests is its complete disregard of their harmful effects on future generations which, according to biologists and physicians, will be the result of the radiation to which we are being exposed.

The declaration signed by the 9,235 scientists did well in stressing the danger.

We must not be responsible for the future birth of thousands of children with the most serious mental and physical defects, simply because we did not pay enough attention to that danger. Only those who have never been present at the birth of a deformed baby, never witnessed the whimpering shock of its mother, dare to maintain that the risk in going on with nuclear tests is one which must be taken under existing circumstances. The well-known French biologist and geneticist Jean Rostand calls the continuation of nuclear tests "the future crime" *(le crime dans l'avenir)*. It is the particular duty of women to prevent this sin against the future. It is for them to raise their voices against it in such a way that they will be heard.

It is strange that so far nobody has stressed that the question of whether nuclear tests should be stopped or continued is not one which concerns the nuclear powers exclusively, a question for them to decide at pleasure. Who is giving these countries the right to experiment, in time of peace, with weapons involving the most serious risks for the whole world? What has international law—enthroned by the United Nations and so highly praised in our time—to say on this matter? Does it no longer look out on the world from its temple? Then take it out that it may face the facts and do its duty accordingly.

International law would at once discover the interesting case of Japan, which suffers heavily from the effects of nuclear tests. The radioactive clouds created by the Soviet tests in North-East Siberia and by the American ones at Bikini in the Pacific Ocean are carried by the winds over Japan. The resulting radioactive poisoning is the worst possible. Very heavily radioactive rainfalls are quite common. The radioactive poisoning of the soil and the vegetation is so powerful that the inhabitants of various districts ought to abstain from using their harvest for food. But they have no alternative but to eat rice infected with strontium, an element particularly dangerous to children. The ocean surrounding Japan is also at times dangerously radioactive, and thereby the very food-supply of the country—in which fish has always played an important part—is being threatened because of the large amount of radioactive fish unsuitable for consumption.

As every new nuclear test makes a bad situation worse, the Japanese government, when hearing of plans for new tests to the north or south of Japan, has presented its country's urgent appeal in Washington or Moscow, beseeching the American or Soviet authorities to give up their plans. The answer was always the same—they regret there can be no question of doing so while as yet the powers have reached no agreement to that effect. As recently as 20th February 1958, this happened again in the capital of one of the nuclear powers.

We always learn about such appeals and their refusal through short paragraphs in the newspaper—just like any other news item. The press does not disturb us with editorials drawing our attention to and making us share in what lies behind such news—the misery of the Japanese people. Thus we and the press are made guilty of lack of compassion. More guilty however is international law, which has kept silent and indifferent on this question, year after year.

It is high time to realize that the question of continuing or ceasing nuclear tests is an urgent matter for international law. Mankind is imperilled by the tests. Mankind insists that they stop, and has every right to do so.

If there is left in the civilization of our times anything of living international law, or if it should be re-established, then the nations responsible for nuclear tests must renounce them immediately, without making this dependent on a disarmament agreement. This matter has nothing to do with disarmament. The nations in question will continue to have those weapons which they now have.

There is no time to lose. New tests increasing the danger must not be allowed to take place. It is important to realize that even without new tests the danger will increase during the coming years: a large part of the radioactive elements flung up in the atmosphere and stratosphere at the nuclear experiments is still there. It will come down only after several years, probably about fifteen.

The immediate renunciation of further tests will create a favorable atmosphere for talks on banning the use of nuclear weapons. When this urgently necessary step has been taken, such negotiations can take place in peace.

That the Soviet Union is now willing to renounce further tests is of great importance. If Britain and the U.S.A. could bring themselves to the same reasonable decision demanded by international law, humanity would be liberated from the fear of being threatened in its existence by the increase of the radioactive poisoning of the air and of the soil resulting from the tests.

---

## THE DANGER OF AN ATOMIC WAR

TODAY we have to envisage the menacing possibility of an out break of atomic war between Soviet Russia and America. It can only be avoided if the two powers decide to renounce atomic arms.

How has this situation arisen?

In 1945 America succeeded in producing an atom bomb with uranium 235. On 6th August 1945, this bomb was released on Hiroshima and on 9th August, on Nagasaki.

America's possession of such a bomb gave her a military advantage over other countries.

In July 1949 the Soviet Union also possessed such a bomb. And its power was equal to the one which was brought into being by America between 1946 and 1949. Consequently peace between the two powers was maintained on the basis of mutual respect for the bomb of the other.

On 3rd October 1952, England exploded its first atom bomb on the Isle of Montebello, on the northwest coast of Australia.

Then, to secure an advantage, America took the decision to invite Edward Teller to produce the hydrogen bomb. It was expected that this H-bomb would exceed many times the power of the uranium bomb. This bomb was first released in May 1951 at Eniwetok on the Pacific atoll Elugelab in October 1952. On 1st March 1954, at Bikini, one of the group in the Marshall Islands in the Pacific Ocean, the perfected H-bomb was exploded. It was found that the actual power of the explosion was much stronger than was originally expected on the basis of calculations.

But at the same time as America, the Soviet Union also started producing H-bombs, the first of which was exploded on 12th August 1953. Both powers progressed contemporaneously. America invented the atom bomb during the second world war, and subsequently worked on the principles of the rockets which served Germany in those days.

War no longer depends on the ability of mighty airplanes to carry bombs to their targets. Now there are guided rockets that can be launched from their starting point and directed with accuracy to a distant target. Missiles are carried by such rockets propelled by a fuel which is constantly being developed in efficiency. The missile carried by the rocket can be an ordinary missile or one which contains a uranium warhead or an H-bomb warhead.

It is said that the Soviet Union certainly disposes of rockets with a range up to 625 miles, and probably with a range up to 1,100 miles.

America is said to possess rockets with a range of 1,500 miles.

Whether the so-called intercontinental missile with a range of 5,000 miles exists cannot be ascertained. It is assumed that the problem of its production is on the way to being solved, and that both East and West are occupied with its production.

Although an intercontinental rocket is not yet known to be completed, America has to be prepared for submarines shooting such a projectile far into the country. These rockets proceed with immense velocity. It is expected that an inter-continental rocket would not take more than half an hour to cross the oceans with loads of bombs from one to five tons.

How would an atomic war be conducted today? At first the so-called local war—but today there is little difference be-tween a local war and a global war. Rocket missiles will be used up to a range of 1,500 miles. The destruction should not be underestimated, even if caused only by a type of Hiroshima bomb, not to speak of an H-bomb.

It can hardly be expected that an enemy will renounce the use of atom bombs, or the most perfected H-bombs, on large cities from the very outset. The H-bomb has a thousand-fold stronger development of power than the atom bomb.

It is therefore quite possible that in a future atomic war both rocket projectiles and large bombers will be used together. Rocket projectiles will not replace bombers, but will rather complement them.

The immediate effect of an H-bomb will have a range of several miles. The heat will be 100 million degrees. One can imagine how great the number of city-dwelling human beings who would be destroyed by the pressure of the explosion, by flying fragments of glass, by heat and fire and by radioactive waves, even if the attack is only of short duration. The deadly radioactive infection, as a consequence of the explosion, would have a range of some 45,000 square miles.

An American general said to some Congressmen: "If at intervals of ten minutes 110 H-bombs are dropped over the U.S.A. there would be a casualty list of about 70 million people, besides some thousands of square miles made useless for a whole generation. Countries like England, West Germany and France could be finished off with 15 to 20 H-bombs."

President Eisenhower has pointed out, after watching maneuvers under atomic attack, that defense measures in a future atomic war become useless. In these circumstances all one can do is to pray.

Indeed, not much more can be done in view of an attack by H-bombs than to advise all people living to hide behind very strong walls of stone or cement, and to throw themselves on the ground and to cover the back of their head, and the body if possible, with cloth. In this way it may be possible to escape annihilation and death through radiation. It is essential that those surviving be given food and drink which are not radioactive and that they be transported away from the radioactive district.

It is impossible to erect walls of such thickness for the whole population of a city. Where would the material and the means come from? How would a population have time even to run to safety in such bunkers?

In an atomic war there would be neither conqueror nor vanquished. During such a bombardment both sides would suffer the same fate. A continuous destruction would take place and no armistice or peace proposals could bring it to an end.

When people deal with atomic weapons, no one can say to the other, "Now the arms must decide"; but only, "Now we want to commit suicide together, destroying each other mutually . . . "

There is good reason for an English M.P. saying, "He who uses atomic weapons becomes subject to the fate of a bee, namely, when it stings it will perish inevitably, for having made use of its sting." He who uses atomic weapons to defend freedom would become subject to a similar fate.

Those who conduct an atomic war for such freedom will die, or end their lives miserably. Instead of freedom they will find destruction. Radioactive clouds resulting from a war between East and West would imperil humanity everywhere. There would be no need to use up the remaining stock of atom and H-bombs. There are about 50,000 of them.

An atomic war is therefore the most senseless and lunatic act that could ever take place. At all costs it must be prevented.

Unfortunately a cold war may turn into an atomic war. This danger is made greater today than it has ever been, because of the possiblity of employing long-distance rockets.

In days gone by America held to the principle of being, apart from the Soviet Union, the sole owner of atomic weapons. There was no virtue in equipping other countries with atom and H-bombs, for they would not have known what to do with them. But, with the arrival of rocket projectiles of a smaller type and a longer range, the situation is changing. The use of such smaller weapons is possible for lesser countries who are in alliance with America. Thus America had deviated from her principle not to put atomic weapons into the hands of other countries, a decision with grave consequences.

On the other hand it is understandable that America wishes to supply the NATO countries with such new weapons for defense against the Soviet Union. The presence of such arms constitutes a new threat to the Soviet Union, opening the way for an atomic war between America and the Soviet Union on European soil. This situation did not exist before. Now the Soviet Union is within range of such rockets from European soil, even as far as Moscow and Kharkov, up to 1,500 miles away.

Rockets of average range could be used for defense purposes by Turkey and Iran against the Soviet Union, into which they could penetrate deeply with such arms accepted from America, and the Soviet Union in turn may now be forced into a situation in which it has to defend itself.

Both America and the Soviet Union may now seek alliances with the Middle East by offering such countries financial support. Such quarrels as may occur could start in secret, and unknown events in the Middle East could endanger the peace of the world.

The risk of an atomic war is being increased by the fact that no warning would be given in starting such a war, which could originate in some mere incident. The side that attacks first would have the initial advantage over the attacked, who would at once sustain losses that would reduce his fighting capacity considerably.

The necessity for a round-the-clock alert against attack carries with it the extreme danger of an error in interpreting what appears on a radar screen, when immediate action is imperative, resulting in the outbreak of an atomic war.

Attention was drawn to this danger by the American General Curtis Le May when recently the world was on the brink of such a situation. The radar stations of the American Air Force and American Coastal Command reported that an invasion of unidentified bombers was on the way. Upon this warning the General in command of the strategic bomber force decided to order a reprisal bombardment to commence. However, realizing the enormity of his responsibility, he then hesitated. Shortly afterwards it was discovered that the radar stations had made a technical error. What could have happened if a less balanced General had been in his place?

In the future such dangers are likely to increase owing to the fact that small rockets exist which pass through the air with terrific speed, and are difficult to identify, so that defense possibilities become very limited. The defense has only seconds in which to identify the approaching rockets and to counterattack by exploding these before they can reach their targets, at the same time dispatching bombers to destroy the ramps from which they are launched.

Such decisions cannot be left to the human brain, for it works too slowly. They have to be entrusted to an electronic brain. If it appears that enemy rockets are really on the way on the radar screen, calculations as to their distance have to be made to the fraction of a second, so that an immediate start can be made by releasing defense rockets.

All this proceeds automatically. Such is our achievement that we now depend entirely on an electronic brain, and on errors and omissions from which such an instrument cannot be exempt. The making of a decision by means of an electronic brain, though quicker, is not as reliable as the making of a decision by the human brain. At some point the complex mechanism of the electronic brain may become faulty.

These developments lead inevitably to a worsening of the situation. We have to reckon with the fact that America may proceed with the supply of atomic weapons to other countries, trusting them not to use them selfishly or incautiously. Both the other atomic powers are at liberty to do likewise.

Yet, who can guarantee that among the favored countries in possession of such weapons there may not be black sheep acting on their own, without regard for the consequences?

Who is to prevent them? Who is able to make them renounce the use of atomic weapons, even if other countries have decided to make such a decision in common? The dam is breached and it may collapse.

That such anxieties have become very real is shown by a statement on the 13th January 1958 on behalf of 9,235 scientists of UNO regarding the cessation of atomic tests. One of their points is the following: "As long as atomic weapons remain in the hands of the three great powers, an agreement as to their control is possible. However, if the tests continue and extend to other countries in possession of atomic weapons, the risks and responsibilities in regard to an outbreak of an atomic war become all the greater. From every point of view the danger in a future atomic war becomes all the more intense, so that an urgent renunciation of atomic weapons becomes absolutely imperative."

America's attitude to the renunciation of atomic weapons is remarkable. It cannot be otherwise—her conviction is that they should be outlawed, yet at the same time in case this does not come about she strives, with other countries in NATO, to put herself in the most favorable military situation. Thus America insists that the rockets which she offers to other countries should be accepted as soon as possible. She seeks to hold such a position as enables her to maintain peace by terrifying her opponent. But she is finding that most of the NATO countries are reluctant to acquire the weapons which they are being offered, because of an increasing strengthening of adverse public opinion.

It would be of immense importance if America in this hour of destiny could decide in favor of renouncing atomic weapons, to remove the possiblity of an eventual outbreak of an atomic war. The theory of peace through terrifying an opponent by a greater armament can now only heighten the danger of war.

A ray of light in darkness—in December 1957 the Polish Foreign Minister Rapacki made a proposition that Czechoslovakia, East and West Germany should consist of an atom-free zone. If this proposal is accepted and the atom-free zones could be enlarged to include adjoining countries the main-

tenance of peace would be assured. The beginning of the end of
the specter that overshadows the Soviet Union would become
an accomplished fact.

With this sensible proposition, public opinion in Europe is
in absolute agreement. It has become convinced, during
recent months, that under no circumstances is Europe to
become a battlefield for an atomic war between the Soviet
Union and America. From this conviction it will no longer
deviate. The time is past when a European country could plan
secretly to establish itself as a great power by manufacturing
atomic weapons exclusively for its own use. Since public opinion would never agree to such an undertaking, it becomes
senseless even to prepare secretly for the realization of such
a plan.

Past too is the time when NATO generals and European
governments can decide on the establishment of launching-
sites and the stockpiling of atomic weapons. The dangers of
atomic war, and its consequences, are now such that these
decisions have ceased to be purely matters of politics and can
be valid only with the sanction of public opinion.

---

## NEGOTIATIONS AT THE HIGHEST LEVEL

WHAT is the position regarding the negotiations that should
lead to the renunciation of nuclear weapons?

One reads and hears that the success of the projected
Summit Conference must depend entirely on its every detail
being diplomatically prepared beforehand. The best diplomacy is objectivity. A fitting preparation would be in sight (if a
respectful and well-meaning criticism is permissible) if the
statesmen and others associated with it would change from
their present undiplomatic way of dealing with each other and
return to a diplomatic method. Many unnecessary, thought-
less, discourteous, foolish and offensive remarks have passed
between them, both in the spoken and written word, to the dis-
advantage of the political atmosphere.

It would be right if, at last, those who have the authority to
take the responsibility, and not those who have only nominal
authority and who cannot move an inch beyond their instruc-

tions, would confer together.

It would be right to go ahead with the conference. For close on four months East and West have talked and written to one another, without any conclusions as to the date and the program being reached. Public opinion everywhere is finding it difficult to accept this state of affairs and is beginning to ask itself whether a conference which so limps into being has any hope of really achieving anything.

It would be right to hold the conference in a town in some neutral European country, for example, Geneva, as was the case in 1955.

It would be right that at this conference only questions that have to do directly with the reununciation of nuclear weapons should be discussed.

It would be right if not too many people were present at the summit meeting. Only the highest personalities of the three nuclear powers, together with their experts and advisers, should take their seats there.

Admission could also be permitted to the representatives of those peoples who—like the NATO countries with America—are concerned in nuclear matters; they could then state their opinion on the decisions that hold such grave consequences also for them.

It would be only in a quite arbitrary manner that other peoples could claim to be present at the summit. Either all would be qualified to be there, or none. In addition, experience teaches that unnecessarily large attendance brings no advantage to a conference.

The Summit Conference therefore is in no way an international or half-international one, even though its decisions are of great importance to the whole of mankind.

The three nuclear powers and they alone must decide, in awareness of their responsibility to their peoples and to all mankind, whether or not they will renounce the testing and the use of nuclear weapons.

As to the planning of the conference, impartiality justifies one remark, which is that to date such planning has been done without objectiveness, and has therefore led nowhere. This leads to the thought that the same outcome could result from the Summit Conference if it were conducted in the same manner.

Wherein lies the difference between the partial and the impartial, the fitting and the unfitting in this matter? It lies in the answer to the question as to the basis on which the three nuclear powers decide whether or not to renounce the testing and the use of nuclear weapons.

The unobjective reply would be that the decision will depend on whether an agreement is reached on disarmament or not. This is false logic. It presumes that there could be an agreement acceptable to both the East and the West on this issue. But previous negotiations have shown that this is not to be expected; they got stuck right at the start because East and West were unable to reach agreement even on the conditions under which such discussions should take place.

The anticipated procedure itself by its very nature is not impartial. It is based on false logic. The two vital issues so essential to the very existence to mankind—the cessation of tests and the disposal of nuclear weapons, cannot be made dependent on the Heavens performing the impossible political miracle that alone could ensure that none of the three nuclear powers would have some objections to a complete agreement on disarmament.

The fact is that the testing and the use of nuclear weapons carry in themselves the absolute reasons for their being renounced. Prior agreement on any other conditions cannot be considered. Both cause the deepest damage to human rights. The tests in so far as they do harm to peoples far from the territories of the nuclear powers, endangering their lives and their health—and this in peace-time; an atomic war in so far as the resulting radioactivity would make uninhabitable the land of peoples not participating in such a war. It would be the most unimaginably senseless and cruel way of endangering the existence of mankind. That is why it dare not become reality.

The three nuclear powers owe it to themselves and to mankind to reach agreement on these absolute essentials without first dealing with prior conditions.

The negotiations about disarmament are therefore not the forerunner of such agreement, but the outcome of it. They start from the point where agreement on the nuclear issues has been reached, and their goal is to reach the point where the three nuclear powers and the peoples who are connected with them must agree on guarantees that will seek to avert the danger of a threat of a non-atomic nature taking the place of the previous danger. Everything that the diplomats will have done objectively to prepare the preliminaries to the conference will keep its meaning even if it will be used not before renunciation, but as a result of it.

Should agreement be reached on the outlawing of nuclear weapons, this alone without any negotiations will have led to a great improvement in the political situation, because as a result of such an agreement time and distance would again become realities with their own rights. Nuclear arms give a distant war the effect of a near war. The Soviet Union and America, in spite of the vast distance that separates them, can menace one another with atomic missiles in so frightful a manner and in so short a space of time, as if they lay next to one another. Having become neighbors, they are in constant fear of their lives every minute.

But if nuclear arms are no longer in question, even the rockets and missiles would not present nearly the same destructive danger. The nearness that endangers existence would have ceased to be. If rockets are no longer nuclear arms, Europe is no longer a battlefield for a distant war which has the effect of a near war between the Soviet Union and America.

Today America with her batteries of nuclear rockets in Europe is present with mighty military power in Europe. Europe has become an in-between land between America and Russia, as if America by some displacement of a continent had come closer to her. But if atomic rockets were no longer in question, this unnatural state of affairs would come to an end. America would again become wholly America; Europe wholly Europe; the Atlantic again wholly the Atlantic Ocean—a sea providing distance in time and space.

In this way could come the beginning of the end of America's military presence in Europe, a presence arising from the two world wars. The great sacrifices that America made for Europe during the second world war, and in the years following it, will not be forgotten; the great and varied help that Europe received from her, and the thanks owing for this, will not be forgotten. But the unnatural situation created by the two world wars that led to a dominating military presence in Europe cannot continue indefinitely. It must gradually cease to exist, both for the sake of Europe and for the sake of America.

Now there will be shocked voices from all sides. What will become of poor Europe if American atomic weapons no longer defend it from within and from without? What will happen if Europe is delivered to the Soviets? Must it then not be prepared to languish in a communist Babylonian form of imprisonment for long years?

Here it should be said that perhaps the Soviet Union is not quite so malicious as to think only of throwing itself on Europe at the first opportunity in order to devour it, and perhaps not quite so unintelligent as to fail to consider whether there would be any advantage in upsetting her stomach with this indigestible meal.

What Europe and the Europeans have to agree about is that they belong together for better or for worse. This is a new historical fact that can no longer be by-passed politically.

Another factor that must be recognized politically is that the question is no longer one of subjugating peoples, but of learning to get along with them mentally and spiritually. A Europe standing on its own has no reason to despair.

Disarmament discussions between the three nuclear powers must concern themselves with guarantees that actual, total and irrevocable disposal of nuclear weapons will be secured. The problem of effective control will also have to be anticipated. Reciprocal agreement will have to be reached on permitting international commissions to investigate on national soil.

One talks of giving aircraft belonging to an international police force the right to fly at medium and high altitudes for purposes of spying. One asks to what extent a land would be willing to subject itself to such control over its own territory.

Unfortunate incidents could easily occur. And what about the power that should be entrusted to such an international control? Even the widest form of such control could never ensure that everywhere and all the time it could not be avoided. In the final analysis East and West are dependent on presupposing a certain reciprocal trust in one another.

This applies also in another matter. As a result of renouncing nuclear arms, the Soviet Union's military might, so far as Europe is concerned, would be less affected than that of America. There would remain to the Soviet the many divisions armed with conventional weapons; with those divisions it could easily overrun the NATO states in Western Europe— particularly Western Germany—without it being possible for anyone to come to their aid. With this in mind, the Soviet Union should agree in the course of disarmament negotiations to reduce her army, and to commit herself never to move against Germany. But here, too, no manner of detailed agreements and internationally guaranteed disarmament agreements would be enough; the parties concerned are still dependent on trusting one another.

But we live in a time when the good faith of peoples is doubted more than ever before. Expressions throwing doubt on the trustworthiness of each other are bandied back and forth. They are based on what happened in the first world war, when the nations experienced dishonesty, injustice and inhumanity from one another. How can a new trust come about? And it must.

We cannot continue in this paralyzing mistrust. If we want to work our way out of the desperate situation in which we find ourselves another spirit must enter into the people. It can only come if the awareness of its necessity suffices to give us strength to believe in its coming. We must presuppose the awareness of this need in all the peoples who have suffered along with us. We must approach them in the spirit that we are human beings, all of us, and that we feel ourselves fitted to feel with each other; to think and to will together in the same way.

The awareness that we are all human beings together has become lost in war and through politics. We have reached the point of regarding each other only as members of a people either allied with us or against us and our approach: prejudice, sympathy or antipathy are all conditioned by that. Now we must rediscover the fact that we—all together—are human beings, and that we must strive to concede to each other what moral capacity we have. Only in this way can we begin to believe that in other peoples as well as in ourselves there will arise the need for a new spirit, which can be the beginning of a feeling of mutual trustworthiness towards each other. The spirit is a mighty force for transforming things. We have seen it at work as the spirit of evil which virtually threw us back, from striving towards a culture of the spirit, into barbarism. Now let us set our hopes on the spirit bringing peoples and nations back to an awareness of culture.

At this stage we have the choice of two risks: the one lies in continuing the mad atomic arms race, with its danger of an unavoidable atomic war in the near future; the other in the renunciation of nuclear weapons, and in the hope that America and the Soviet Union, and the peoples associated with them, will manage to live in peace. The first holds no hope of a prosperous future; the second does. We must risk the second.

In President Eisenhower's speech following the launching of the Sputnik on 7th November 1957, he said, "What the world needs more than a gigantic leap into space is a gigantic leap into peace." This gigantic leap consists in finding the courage to hope that the spirit of good sense will arise in individuals and in peoples, a spirit sufficiently strong to overcome the insanity and the inhumanity.

If negotiations on disarmament are held, not as a preliminary to the renunciation of nuclear arms but as a result of it, they would have a much larger meaning. They would be a big step in the direction of finally liquidating the confused situation that followed from the second world war.

Disarmament and all questions leading to a stable situation—such as for example the reunification of East and West Germany—could be discussed much better after agreement had been reached on the renunciation of atomic weapons. A later conference could also deal with many issues left unresolved in the peace treaties after the second world war.

Once agreement on renunciation of nuclear arms had been reached it would be the responsibility of the United Nations to ensure that now as in the future they would be neither made nor used. The danger that one nation or another might hit on the idea of manufacturing nuclear weapons will have to be borne in mind for some considerable time. We must consider ourselves lucky that they are not yet in the possession of other peoples somewhere in the world.

The problem of how far disarmament and renunciation of all weapons can go will have to be investigated, because the second world war showed what terrible destruction conventional weapons can cause, destruction which the development of rockets has potentially vastly increased. One wishes that agreement could be reached immediately to renounce rockets and missiles, but this can only come as a result of a spiritual advance everywhere which as yet it is difficult to visualize.

Of all the very difficult problems the future holds, the most difficult will be the rights of access of over-populated countries to neighboring lands. But if in our time we renounce nuclear arms we shall have taken the first step on the way to the distant goal of the end to all wars. If we do not do this we remain on the road that leads in the near future to atomic war and misery.

Those who are to meet at the Summit must be aware of this, so that they can negotiate with propriety, with an adequate degree of seriousness and with a full sense of responsibility. The Summit Conference must not fail: public opinion will not this time accept failure to agree on the renunciation of nuclear weapons which is so essential to peace.

*Letters*

# 5

# Letters to Norman Cousins

*In the 1950s, Norman Cousins—then editor of **The Saturday Review (of Literature)**—published several articles on Albert Schweitzer, one defending him against criticisms of his hospital in Africa.*[1] *They also had several mutual friends.*

*As the public controversy on the wisdom of nuclear weapons tests escalated and soon reached world-wide dimensions, Cousins became a leader of the movement to end nuclear tests, especially in North America. Cousins realized that Schweitzer would be an important ally. Cousins visited Lambaréné in January 1957 and Schweitzer promised to issue a statement against nuclear testing. After Cousins left Africa, a correspondence between the two— which originated earlier—grew and remained intense for several years, and continued if less frequently until Schweitzer's death.*

*The contents of this correspondence were not published until Cousins in 1985 issued **Albert Schweitzer's Mission: Healing and Peace**. The letters reproduced in the following chapter do not constitute all those found in Cousins' book. The text of Cousins' letters are, for reasons only of space, also not given. They can be found, however, in Cousins' volume. Acknowledgement is made to Norman Cousins for permission to reprint these letters.*

FEBRUARY 23, 1957[2]

Lambaréné
February 23, 1957

To Norman Cousins

Dear friend,

Let us talk now about the question of the declaration which has to be made about the subject of the atomic bomb tests. I worked rather hard on the question about the tests and how to write a statement. If you really think that I could do something useful I will do it, as tired as I am. . . .

So I return to the idea of having my message spread by radio, as a message by radio can be heard over the whole world. But to which radio can the mission of the publication be charged, without others feeling indisposed? Answer: Radio Oslo, of the city of the Nobel Peace Prize! That my voice departs from there where I delivered my address of the Nobel Peace Prize will be found justifiable and reasonable. In my message I will humbly ask the radio stations of other countries to broadcast it too, and to consider addressing it to humanity.

I am on good terms with the president of the Commission of the Nobel Peace Prize, and with Norwegian radio. I was happy to find this solution. If you approve of it, please cable me: "Hospital Schweitzer. Lambaréné. Agree with you." (You can cable this in English.) If you feel you must make objections, please write me as soon as possible. I am fortunate and grateful to have you as an adviser.

But, all this remains between you and me!

Heartily, yours devotedly,
Albert Schweitzer

---

APRIL 22, 1957[3]

Lambaréné, Gabon
April 22, 1957

To Norman Cousins

Dear friend:

Excuse the poor creature that I am for not having been

able to send you the text of the speech earlier, as I would have liked to do. But time was pressing. I had to send it as quickly as possible to the president of the Nobel Prize Committee in Oslo so that he could decide if he could take the responsibility to ask the Norwegian radio network to undertake the great task of approaching the directors of radio networks of different nations so they would agree to broadcast it. These preparations had to be done in less than three weeks! . . .

What's essential is that what was due to your initiative has succeeded and that the attempt to awaken the attention of humanity to the subject of the danger that atomic bomb tests already convey for human existence is being undertaken under the best of conditions, thanks to the Nobel Prize Committee and the Norwegian radio. This appeal had to come from a completely neutral place. This was the great problem. In reality, UN should have been the one to undertake the matter. But it is an organization that functions in complicated ways. Perhaps it is better that the UN will not undertake it and that this is a spontaneous movement which is manifested outside the UN . . .

From my heart, your devoted<br>Albert Schweitzer

---

MAY 5, 1957[4]

Lambaréné, Gabon<br>May 5, 1957

Norman Cousins

Dear friend,

. . . I knew that April 20th was the right psychological moment and asked Oslo to make the impossible possible. What the Nobel Committee and Radio Oslo managed to achieve in three weeks is magnificent. One hundred and fifty transmitters throughout the world broadcast the address in the East, in Asia, Australia, South America . . . these are all of value to me. It must reach the point where there is an open public opinion among mankind; that is why the address had to have as wide a range as possible. Also it must have been generally understandable: that is why it appears to have been written by a shoemaker. It was with intent that I restricted myself to the cessation of atomic tests. One must have the right beginning. And right at the end I spoke quite quietly of the political and diplomatic side, and of the need to encourage that aspect by means of an open public opinion. But I don't count much on that . . . Now oftentimes I think of you. Without your coming here I don't think I should have decided to make the statement. You were right to encourage me to do it. I will not forget that. . . .

So *aufwiedersehen.* If you have anything interesting about the nuclear situation please send it on to me. You can write in English; I can read it well. . . .

Cordially yours,<br>Albert Schweitzer

---

OCTOBER 14, 1957[5]

Dr. Albert Schweitzer<br>Günsbach<br>Haut-Rhin<br>France<br>October 14, 1957

Mr. Norman Cousins

Dear friend:

I've been following the debates at the United Nations on disarmament with great attention. I find it sad that Henry Cabot Lodge, deputy of the United States of America, declares in his speech that the nuclear explosions do not present a grave danger. He makes a very bad impression on the entire world in relying on a theory which real scholars and physicians recognize as absolutely false, especially in view of the disastrous effects for human beings still to be born. I wonder if American scholars and physicians can accede to it without protesting against an American representative who professes such a false opinion in the name of America. . . . It's up to them to decide if they will tolerate it or not. One could think that it would be better that the protest came from them than from abroad. What a sad time we're living in! Falsehood rises up in the name of facts against truth, while the latter cannot manifest itself as it should because the lie is joined with well-organized publicity.

What will be the result of the United Nations debates? Considering how they're engaged now, there is little hope that they will arrive at a solution. . . . Congratulate Stassen and Flanders on my behalf if you have the chance. I think a great deal about them these days. . . .

But treat the contents of my letter as completely personal. I don't want to give the impression that I am meddling in U.S.A. affairs.

> From my heart, your devoted
> Albert Schweitzer

---

NOVEMBER 11, 1957[6]

> Lambaréné, Gabon
> November 11, 1957

Mr. Norman Cousins

Dear friend,

. . . it is necessary that . . . unofficial public opinion has an absolutely American origin and a completely American character. Otherwise its enemies could diminish its importance, saying that it was inspired from abroad. That would be very grave. American opinion must pronounce itself with complete sovereignty on the situation that has been created at present by my Declaration—insofar as American opinion is known, it does not yet allow for this new situation, but in a general sense it contains the spirit of this new unofficial attitude. It asks for the suspension of nuclear tests as a first act. But one could say that it was I who asked for this first step, and that it is not the people in America alone who proclaim it. I attach great importance to the fact that the Russian proposal calling for a meeting of American and Russian scientists goes back to something inspired by Cyrus Eaton a year ago. . . . The strength of the manifestation of this unofficial opinion lies in the fact that it is completely American. Avoid everything that could attenuate this characteristic; encourage that which will enable it to become popular. Reflect well on this and you will see that I am right. That Americans come out against the opinion of American politics is the beginning of the beginning. And a general movement in Europe could grow out of that example. Once things are that far I could then help in the creation of the general movement, if I judge that my intervention could serve a purpose. The fire must be lighted in the U.S.A., and I will then be able to help other men of other lands to bring the wood to throw onto the fire and to give it the importance it should have to enable it to create a different atmosphere. All this between ourselves. Sustain the movement in America and it will propagate itself in Europe, and in the world. And count on me for everything that I will be able to do to propagate the movement.

From the heart, your devoted
Albert Schweitzer

---

December 12, 1957[7]

Lambaréné, Gabon
December 12, 1957

Mr. Norman Cousins

Dear friend,

I'm writing you from the ship "Brazza" on which I'm returning to Lambaréné. We are south of Dakar. If I'm writing you so late . . . it's that I had an accident, a fracture of a bone in the right hand in mid-September, and it's taking a long time to heal. Writing still demands an effort and I have to be very careful with this hand. I've been following events with full attention as much as I can. I believe you must be pleased with the echo found by your appeal to reason. I particularly appreciated the opinion expressed by the former American ambassador to the U.S.S.R. This testimony has particular importance. Now we must await the results of the Paris meeting. It is very interesting that Chancellor Adenauer has spontaneously declared that he would not consider the question of installations for American weapons on German territory as an actuality. Norway and Denmark also have the same attitude. This means that the Paris conference will not succeed in mobilizing Europe. What is curious is that England has declared herself ready to receive American nuclear weapons on her territory without waiting until the Paris conference takes place. I don't know whether the news that Sweden and France want to build nuclear arms has real foundation. Given the French financial situation, one wonders how she can find means for this enterprise. . . . Thus we must wait to see how the situation works out in Paris. But I would judge that the decisions will be less serious than one would have feared a little while ago.

Concerning this you can inform me about what is happening in the United States; this would be of great service to me. I admire you for all you've undertaken and succeeded in. You've created a movement that did not exist before. When will we see each other again? I won't forget you. With my best wishes.

Your devoted
Albert Schweitzer

---

APRIL 14, 1958[8]

April 14, 1958

Mr. Norman Cousins,

Dear friend,

At last, you are receiving the appeals which you have been expecting for a long time. There are three appeals, each for a different night. They were finished as early as mid-March. But then came the negotiating with Oslo because I inquired if they intended again to broadcast my appeals. After all, there is a certain significance in the fact that they are broadcast from Oslo, the seat of the Parliamentary Commission for the Nobel Peace Prize. Oslo is very kind and will do it again although the three appeals are much more political than last year's appeal. Then there were negotiations about the date. Oslo will now broadcast the three appeals on April 28, 29, and 30. Before that time they must not be disseminated anywhere by newspapers or radio—I had to make this promise to Oslo. You must therefore keep the text in a safe place so that nobody can pass it on to the press or radio.

I am sending you the first appeal in the English translation which I received from Oslo. As to the other two appeals, you will have to arrange for them to be translated there. So, on April 28, you may give the texts to the newspapers and to the radio if you have a station at your disposal, and later you may do anything you like.

The text is intended for Europe where we have to keep the NATO generals from forcing launching pads and nuclear weapons on the governments, which would amount to a military isolation of the Soviet Union and which could lead to war. We cannot and will not tolerate this NATO domination, which does not at all consider the abolition of nuclear weapons but only the continuation of armament. What is also on our minds is that the military presence of America in Europe which was brought about by the two world wars is unnatural and must gradually come to an end. This question has become an issue already because America by resisting the abolition of nuclear weapons exposes Europe to the danger of becoming the battlefield of a nuclear war between the Soviet Union and America. But sooner or later this idea of a slow emancipation of Europe from American weapons would have come up anyway. It has been in the air since the creation of NATO, which exercises military power over Europe, and especially since NATO has wanted to force nuclear weapons on us. America's wrong policy on nuclear weapons has triggered off this development. It is necessary that America's rulers take note of this and take it into account. We no longer wish to be associated with the idea that America keeps the free world free by the threat of a nuclear war. This theory fails to appreciate the meaning of a nuclear war with contemporary arms. But I talk with affection about the U.S.A. and the help she has given Europe. If you think a phrase about the U.S. policy on nuclear weapons is too strong for the American readers and listeners, just leave it out. The same applies to all three appeals. But the American government may know that public opinion does not agree with its policy on nuclear weapons for NATO and that it puts pressure on the European governments from which they cannot escape.

My third appeal deals in detail with the top-level negotiations. I hold the opinion that nuclear weapons are against international law and that they have to be abolished for that reason irrespective of whether or not the three atomic powers have come to a satisfactory disarmament agreement, because in peace and in war they harm the uninvolved people and even humanity. I think this thesis will be considered important during the top-level negotiations. If the abolition of nuclear weapons is not achieved during these top-level negotiations, we will be in a serious situation. . . .

Please regard this letter as strictly personal. If you write to me about your opinion on the three appeals, I shall be pleased. I worked hard on them during the nights.

Devotedly,
Albert Schweitzer

---

MAY 17, 1958[9]

Lambaréné, Gabon
May 17, 1958

Norman Cousins

Dear friend,

Finally I am writing to you. I am still very tired by the work on the three appeals for which I had to read many newspaper articles in small print and to make excerpts from them. My eyes have suffered from this. Sometimes now they refuse to work. Also my hand is exhausted and refuses sometimes to serve me. However, more important is that the appeals catch the attention of people and awake them. And how good it is that I was allowed to use Radio Oslo, and by it a hundred radio stations in the world, for the atomic issue. The whole enterprise did not cost a cent. It is incredible.

Now my opinion on your plans. I do not agree that we should appeal to the International Court in The Hague. First, it deals only with governments and not with private persons. Second, if ever it should make a sentence or an expert statement, it would be expressed in judicial language full of clauses, with the effect that nobody would know what to think of it. It would not be of any use in the struggle against atomic arms. The lawyers would have been the ones to use and raise the argument that atomic weapons contradict the law of humanity; but they were silent and have failed. Therefore we will leave them out of the game. They would be but unreliable allies. Keep away from lawyers, keep away from courts. . . .

Also the Pope we will leave alone. He is a great sir, and he owes consideration to the Church. He may be a good man, but he is no fighter. Or did you ever read anywhere that he condemned the atomic and H bombs in the name of Christian religion? Protestantism does it, but there is no Catholic declaration so far. . . .

My opinion is to group the whole thing about the International Court in The Hague. If this court were efficient it would raise its voice by itself. But it is not allowed to do so. It is allowed only to judge complaints brought before it by governments. My hope is that among the lawyers in the world there will be some to open their mouths.

Our purpose in expressing the argument that atomic weapons contradict international law is to arm the hands of the opponents of atomic weapons, or their mouths, in order that they may shout it all over the world. It is evident that atomic weapons are contrary to international law. People will believe it because of its evidence and because it is based on human and moral reflections. We don't need the lawyers' blessings. History shows how it is their role to pour water into the neat wine of the law of humanity and to construct compromises.

Our task is to raise our voices permanently in order to awake those who are still asleep and to build up a public opinion which is capable of bearing pressure upon the governments, as is happening already in Germany.

And just because in my appeals this argument—that atomic weapons contradict international law—is mentioned over and over again, I want it to be published in a paperback booklet with the title *Peace or Atomic War?* in many countries. I ask you to find a good courageous publisher for it in the U.S.A. I had written previously to you about this in the beginning. It is difficult for me to do this from Europe. You can believe me that the appeals will have their best effect only after being spread to the people, in an inexpensive edition. Magazines and groups must be allowed to reprint them at low costs. If you have a publisher tell him to send me at once a contract for me to sign. I want 8 percent of the price as royalties (of the price in shop sale). It has to be quite a simple, cheap edition. The sooner it is published the better. Don't lose much time. Another thing. You can tell your friends that I do not think much of an appeal to the International Court in The Hague, and that I will not join it; and also that I do not think it the right thing to contact the Pope; the Pope should speak in his own way against atomic weapons. So much you may tell your friends. But the reasons for this opinion of mine they need not know, and should not quote them in public. I am fighting against the atomic danger; but it is not up to me to judge the lawyers and the Pope.

With best thoughts<br>A.S.

P.S. Radio and the press are the small firewood to kindle a fire; booklets which are passed from one hand to the next are the big logs to keep the fire burning and to bring it to its full effect.

---

AUGUST 15, 1958[10]

Lambaréné, Gabon<br>August 15,1958

Norman Cousins

Dear friend,

I take the opportunity while I am writing to Erica [Anderson], also to write a letter to you, especially about the nuclear situation, which quieted down because the newspapers are occupied with the adventure of Dulles and Macmillan in the

Middle East. But that does not mean that all is well. On the contrary. This unexpected and senseless sending of troops to the Middle East has shown the people in Europe that the danger of an atomic war, which can start at any time, really exists, and it has shaken the authority very considerably of the two statesmen, who count this danger as small, especially so in Germany. And the people have had to admit that Khrushchev kept calm and that he did not answer the unnecessary sending of troops with sending troops on his part. This led many people to think about the question, whether the free world is really so much endangered by the Soviets as it is being preached all over the West. And that neither the U.S.A. nor England thought it necessary to let the other countries belonging to NATO know about their decided adventure has harmed the reputation of NATO very much, again especially in Germany. That the U.S.A. and England took such a long time to arrive at an agreement with Russia for the taking place of a conference about the Middle East situation has brought about an estrangement in Europe, and that it has given Red China an opportunity and time to force Russia also to talk in its name, is being judged as a very bad thing indeed, because the mixing Chinese politics into Middle East politics and also into European situations is a fact of which one cannot foresee the results. You do remember that I have written to you for quite a while that Khrushchev has a difficult time with China and that America and England should take this to heart and not make more difficulties. Now, what could have been avoided has happened, become fact. Through America's refusal to recognize the real government of China, the situation does not get easier. There is now an uneasiness in Europe that the policy of Dulles is not satisfactory. That American newspapers criticize him very much also makes an impression in Europe. All this brings with it that those who plead for the use of atomic weapons do not have the authority now as they used to. What is important is that the argument that atomic weapons are against the law of the people (Völkerrecht) finds more and more recognition, and that the meaning of this is being well understood. Recently I received from a lawyer of a German university an article, which he has published in an important newspaper. In this article, he proves legally that all weapons which produce radioactivity, *even those which are being praised as clean,* have to be looked on as opposed to the "Völkerrecht" and must be abandoned. I will try to send you a copy of this article. Until now the lawyers have shied away from questions that were unsympathetic to the governments; they have just not lived up to occupying themselves with this. But now, when everywhere this question has been discussed, they cannot do otherwise but to occupy themselves with it. Whenever I could I have in letters talked about this argument that atomic weapons are against the laws of the people. . . . So calmly and confidently carry on with the battle. . . . Write much about it and open your mouth. That is better than to hold many conferences . . . and cheaper. . . .

Your devoted,
A.S.

---

AUGUST 24, 1958[11]

August 24, 1958

Mr. Norman Cousins

Dear friend,

How beautiful that I received the good news, especially through you! I was sitting just then at the table in my room when Mlle. Mathilde came and said: Just now a telegram arrived with a very wonderful message. Then she put it in front of me. I read it with deep emotion. And then I looked at the table next to me, at which you, at your first visit here, were sitting, when you tried to convince me that I should speak in regard to atomic weapons. Before, others had talked to me, asked me to do so, without my being able to make a decision. Then you came and asked me the same and it impressed me. So it was you who made me do it, to take up the word for the cause. I remember well the letter in which I told you and also the letter I received from you, your kind answer. Our pact in Lambaréné has surely contributed to the fact that the powers possessing atomic weapons had to give in, at least as regards this question. And Radio Oslo has also a great merit. That the director of

Radio Oslo, Mr. Fostervoll, and the president of the Parliamentary Commission of the Nobel Peace Committee mustered up enough courage (and courage it needed) to give me permission to speak, in complete freedom, through their radio station has given our opinion in the public eye a great esteem. And moreover, Radio Oslo had moved 90 other stations in the world, at the same time, to make my appeals known, which caused great notice everywhere.

And then, after the first success of our pact followed months in which we changed between fear and hope, because the American "calming" propaganda, with Teller and Strauss and the Atomic Energy Commission had such a terrific success in America and in Europe, that public opinion was chloroformed and the press was apathetic. It meant a lot that Pauling was successful in getting a manifesto from 9,326 scientists, which, in a certain sense, instead of the UN Commission of scientists (who until August 1958 were condemned to silence), put forth an opinion that was sent to the UN—all this, despite the president of the UN burying it in a drawer and letting it lie there.... Yet it made an impression. And then Strauss and Teller made such blunders that Dulles could not hold with them anymore.... And still the press remained apathetic and public opinion did not know how to decide, and did not want to make decisions. That the Soviets renounced the tests was put down as propaganda and made hardly any impression. It mattered greatly that your magazine again and again backed the truth.

On the boat which carried me back to Africa, in the middle of December 1957, I decided to take up the word again and this time to occupy myself also with the political aspects of the problem, as well as the political situation and how this situation had developed. To begin with, Radio Oslo did not want to cooperate in my expression of somewhat temperamental (*temperamentvoller Weise*) views. But when the two gentlemen had read the three appeals, they changed their minds and gave permission so that the appeals would be sent over the stations unaltered. Again Radio Oslo was able to get 90 other stations to publicize these appeals simultaneously, all over the world.

This happened on the 28th, 29th, and 30th of April, a year

after the first appeal (23rd of April 1957). Since it was quite clear to me that in the atomic nations as well as in the NATO countries everything to repress these appeals would be done, in radio as well as in the press, I undertook the big task of trying to place these appeals under the title *Peace or Atomic War?* in as many countries as possible in book form. In this respect my publishers in all countries helped me greatly. So, during the course of four months the appeals became known in America and in Europe, partly through the aid given by your magazine and also through the help of others which published parts of the appeals in short or long form. Much good work was done by the courageous and knowledgeable Pauling, who kept questioning Teller and did not rest until it was proved that, in regard to the underground explosion in Las Vegas on September 19, 1957, a seismograph as far as Alaska *had* registered the disturbance—contrary to what was said at the time. Teller was the bad spirit to which President Eisenhower and Dulles had bowed. He was the one who influenced them to shatter the London conference, which had been going along all right, under the direction of Stassen, during July 1957. He had made them think that by continuing the tests one would arrive at the production of a "clean" hydrogen bomb, which would have no radioactive fallout and which would not hurt civilians. That it was necessary for Dulles to separate himself from Teller refuted the "calming" propaganda, which had tried to create the idea of an idyllic atomic war as well as the fiction of "purity of air" with the new tests.

Later the slogan appeared in America and in Europe simultaneously that one *must* be able to live with the atomic bomb and that one *can* live with the atomic bomb.

Generals and philosophers let this message be spread in the world and public opinion let itself be impressed with it. But the saner statesmen began to understand that they must follow their consciences and resist the movement to continue the tests.

That the conference called by scientists of both East and West agreed that test explosions, even small ones, could not happen without their being noticed opened the way for President Eisenhower to announce that the United States would discontinue these tests. England could not do differently.

How sad, though, that it took so long for these two states to come to this conclusion! To listen to the voice of reason and humanity! A real joy, to have been victorious, cannot rise within us, who have fought the battle of reason and humanity. . . . The disaster which has overcome the world because of the powerful explosions held up till now fills us with sadness, in which there is no room for contentment because of the success finally appearing on the horizon.

Again, we have to keep on fighting the battle for the abolition of the tests . . .

                    With my best thoughts, your devoted
                    A.S.

P.S. When I received your telegram I thought of Einstein—what it would have meant to him if he could have lived to see the day which he longed for so much! As the best answer to your telegram it seemed to me I should give a short report on paper of the developments in the battle in which we are standing together. When will I do the same for the coming second part of the battle?

---

SEPTEMBER 24, 1958[12]

                                September 24, 1958

Norman Cousins

Dear friend,

Your friendly writing in answer to my description of our fight against the test explosions has deeply moved me. But you must not regard my cooperation as something so extraordinary. Each of us has done what he could, be it in Europe or in the U.S.A. For this reason we were able at last to create a public opinion which forced the politicians to capitulate. The opinion of the scientists in Geneva allowed them to capitulate with dignity, but it is a sad thing that the scientists of the West did not have the courage to say that the tests must be stopped on account of the scientific reports. They were forced by their governments to take that attitude, to leave the decision to the politicians. It does not give honor to the West that its scientists were resigned to leaving the verdict to the politicians and not to expressing their views based on scientific findings.

A thousand thanks for the information about the President in these matters. It does hurt one that the U.S.A. will continue the tests until the 31st of October. The terrible storms in Mexico are a result of these tests, I assume. It is strange that all nations accept these storms, which are resulting from the atomic tests, without complaining. But the politicians have been able through the propaganda they started to stop any questions about these atmospheric disturbances of our time, as much as they have been able to silence the lawyers who would deal with the question of atomic weapons in regard to international law. The politicians have also succeeded in preventing people from knowing how great is the amount of damage that has already been done. . . . Everywhere a surface view and lies against which the public opinion does not dare to stand up. Public opinion cannot do anything because the press which should deal with these things does not dare to pick up the word. One cannot understand how humanity keeps on living under these circumstances. They know they are kept in ignorance in regard to the radioactive dangers but they accept this because the press—which should discuss these questions—has failed to bring them up.

And it is our culture which tolerates these circumstances, and does not acquire any knowledge because those who reign feel uncomfortable about it—they don't like to be open about it, they don't allow the public to know the truth about the dangers of the atomic age. These are strange circumstances under which we live . . . and the people in general do not ask themselves to account for all this. I write as many letters as I possibly can to shake the public from their sleep and to clarify for them that the atomic danger concerns not only Europe but all nations. In South America I have had success with these letters and with the publication of *Peace or Atomic War?* The main thing now is to distribute as widely as possible the idea that the atomic weapons are against international law, because the cessation of atomic weapons can only be achieved with this argument.

With loving thoughts your devoted
Albert Schweitzer

NOVEMBER 24, 1958[13]

November 24, 1958

Norman Cousins

Dear friend:

I must tell you how right you were to send an open letter to Geneva. It was necessary that the world hear that a cessation of test explosions was still discussed, that a discussion about the cessation of nuclear weapons production was still going on. The political happenings of recent times have pushed the atomic question completely into the background, which is a fact of great value to those who are pro-atom. It is indeed very sad, as I have written to you already, that the atomic question steps back behind political questions; contributing to this surely has been the political adventure of Dulles in the Middle East and also that in the China Sea. The atom question became a dish of soup which one removes from the table to warm up in the kitchen. And again propaganda dared to advocate holding on to atomic weapons, trying to calm public opinion.

Typical of this is the talk of air protection in the case of an atomic attack. In England, such a paper was published (from the government) which, with photographs, tries to show that there could be *millions of survivors!* Also in Germany the same melody is being heard. It is incredible. . . .

A new political happening has to be cited: Macmillan, Adenauer, and de Gaulle want, together, to put up a war-ready Europe, and encircle the Soviets in this manner. At the moment they do this by making propaganda for a better organized NATO and by suggesting that NATO prepare itself for an atomic war. The original aim of NATO in Europe was to form a force with *ordinary weapons* which could confront the force of the Soviets. But this plan was abandoned because England needed to minimize its army on account of the cost, aiming towards having a professional army rather than a people's army. This the government declares quite openly, however incredible this is. It promises an early halt to compulsory military service, which is only possible if the arming is entirely reduced to atomic weapons. The army of France does not count, because it is, to such an extent, needed in Algeria. The German army, because still small, is also supposed to be modernized with atomic weapons, as far as possible. Belgium reduces military service to one year. So NATO has arrived at a point where only an atomic war is being considered. But atomic weapons are not defenses . . . they are aggressive. Russia's situation is that it has given up its tests in March, probably because of a great accident which has happened during its last tests. During the fall it had to realize that the U.S.A., in the production of tactical small atomic weapons in its tests, has made great progress. Therefore Russia made up its mind to go as far, also to make tests again. Through this, it has now lost the prestige it had gained through its cessation of tests. On the other hand, Dulles, because of his two military adventures (of which the second is in no way finished), has also lost influence in the world. The one thing balances the other a little. A good factor is that the scientists in Geneva, those from the U.S.A. as well as those from Russia, agree as far as the danger is concerned—that is, a mounting radioactivity in the atmosphere. This is the basis for public opinion in the world. This opinion we have to create, everywhere, and we have to back it with the argument that atomic weapons are against international law. This is the road on which we may succeed.

Now the new happenings in Europe. The Soviets continue to follow their policy to avoid being encircled. This has to be taken very seriously now. A great rocket base exists in Italy; very important bases also in Germany. Now Khrushchev intends to retaliate by needling the European powers in every way possible. A genial shikan [to make angry, to bother, to needle] he withdraws the Soviet troops from Germany and then he leaves the supervision of all the powers which have their troops in Germany to East Germany. Now the U.S.A. and England are forced to discuss everything which concerns Berlin, and the territories which have so far been supervised by the Russians, with the East Germans, which until now have not been recognized. This is a great humiliation for them, especially for Adenauer. I believe that the silly word by Dulles, that Berlin is the Quemoy of Europe, is responsible for Khrushchev's action. He wants to show that Berlin is something quite different than Quemoy. How this whole situation will clarify itself cannot be predicted now. Naturally this is a very unfriendly action on the part of Khrushchev, not a bit suited to helping the situation in which we live. The pact which Adenauer and de Gaulle are making is not helping either. De Gaulle's plan to give France atomic weapons and the fact that Adenauer wishes atomic weapons from NATO for his army cause Khrushchev to show Europe that this opposition to the Russians could have grave disadvantages.

In Germany in recent years opinion has spread that one has to tie in with East Germany. This opinion will now become stronger. The public opinion for Adenauer is not quite as strong as two years ago. This is the situation today. The main thing is that the Geneva conference express their opinion clearly. Then one will see further and act specially and fight. It is interesting that Adenauer during the last few days, in a speech, uttered, as an accusation towards Khrushchev, that what he now does in regard to Berlin is *against international law*. This was not very wise. Because with much more reason one can declare that the arming of the German troops is against international law. But it is good that Adenauer commits himself, publicly, to international law.

All this I write to you completely confidentially. But I thought that it would be interesting for you to look at the situation as it appears from the European viewpoint. And again: The address you sent to the conference in Geneva was a very valuable undertaking. It was a declaration which made the world conscious of the fact that the atomic question exists, a question with which public opinion has to occupy itself. Despite all the political happenings which have pressed themselves into the foreground, the nuclear question demands prior attention.

From my heart,
A.S.

---

DECEMBER 4, 1958[14]

Lambaréné
December 4, 1958

Norman Cousins
Dear friend,
   I am glad that you go to Europe. But I don't believe that it

will help to see the heads of governments. The president of Germany is in the same position as the Queen of England: he does not control politics. The politics are being handled entirely by Chancellor Adenauer. For this reason the president avoids talking to anyone, except his intimates, about politics. He would resent it if I asked him to receive you. With Adenauer it is like this: He does not want to talk to anyone. He can bear only people who speak according to his opinion. He feels that many in Germany, concerning the two great problems which are being discussed, do not agree with him and demand that he does not accept atomic weapons from NATO. This worsens the relationship with Russia. They also want him to take up the existing Berlin problems. This public opinion creates great worries in him, more than he is willing to admit. And in me he sees the big enemy, who, because I enjoy great respect in Germany, contributes to this public opinion. Before that, we had a very good relationship with each other. But now I would not dare to visit him because it would cause him pain, and I dare even less to ask him that he see someone whom I recommend.

Altogether I would try, in your place, to contact other persons in Germany. From the outside, one cannot too well influence things in Germany. The Germans want to solve these things by themselves. I am looked upon as a German, in spite of my being a French citizen, on the basis of the Versailles Treaty. But a foreigner can do nothing in Germany. He could only make people who are against Adenauer's nuclear policies and against his East-West policies more antagonistic and in this way give the impression that he is being influenced from the outside. Because the Germans were under foreign sovereignty they are resentful of everything foreign.

You will remember how I refused to step into the anti-atom movement with my name, in the U.S.A. The same principle holds everywhere. In England, they became very resentful for this reason. The Rev. Niemoeller has participated in anti-nuclear domonstrations. We who fight against nuclear weapons must remain in contact all over the world. But the fight in one's own country has to be fought by each one in one's own country.

Don't forget that you are always welcome in Lambaréné!!!
Here we can talk with each other. Here you can rest.
From my heart,
your devoted
Albert Schweitzer

---

MARCH 3, 1959[15]

Lambaréné
March 3, 1959

Dear friend:

Forgive me for not writing sooner. Not only do I have much work to do but I suffer deeply from exhaustion. Also, I must once again take care of my hand that suffers from writer's cramp. Otherwise it might become quite unusable.

That which we are experiencing in the world is sad. How much harm the military undertakings in the Middle East and in Quemoy have done to the cause of stopping nuclear testing. And how much harm they have done to the work in relation to the whole nuclear issue, because they have forced it into the background and have created an atmosphere unsuitable for negotiations. And now we have the question of Berlin added to it all. And that has ruined the atmosphere. The Berlin question gives the politicans who are the virtuosi of madness an opportunity to withdraw from the nuclear issue. They also never stop to ask themselves whether it is morally right to risk an atomic war over the Berlin question. I wonder how many people are really prepared to die because of Berlin. But I still believe that the negotiations to end atomic tests will end well. Most of the difficulties were overcome before the talks were broken off. I believe that no atomic power would now dare to start testing again. Of course that would mean that the peoples of the earth would be aroused and would no longer be prepared to subject themselves to such danger. And we have no reason not to continue our fight against atomic weapons, even under present unfavorable conditions. *We must carry on with our new argument that they are against human rights.* I believe that in this regard much too little has been undertaken. I have been following the various congresses. None of them have taken the position that these arms are against human rights. That the press remains indifferent also in this issue is quite natural, but we, the fighters, must keep shouting about it. The professor of the University of Münster also made the point that such arms violate natural law. Because the press is silent, it is we who must bring this point to bear at the meetings and congresses and *we must stress the legal moral argument.* The human rights declaration was based not only on legal but also on moral grounds, and it is for moral reasons that we must make our stand against extinction. *The fact that law is based on morality is the decisive thing in this case and must be brought to the fore.* Only if we keep stressing these facts can we fight the good fight, can we arouse public opinion—a public opinion that is common to all peoples. That must now be our only goal—to create this enlightened and cohesive public opinion. It is in this arena that the battle must be joined. Otherwise, our cause will not be successful. Could you not publish the Münster professor's talk in your journal? It would be good if such a sensible jurist could be the means of an open debate such as took place as a result of his talk in the German press.

The great anxiety I feel about the issue which we are fighting together causes me to write you in this way. I had hoped to see you in Lambaréné and I go on hoping.

Heartily,
Albert Schweitzer

---

OCTOBER 10, 1961[16]

Lambaréné, Gabon
October 10, 1961

Mr. Norman Cousins

Dear friend:

I have just received your letter of October 2. I make hast

to write these lines to tell you that you are much too pessimistic! The question of Berlin is basically very simple. Basically it is a question of formalities. Until now, the Allies were obliged to notify the Russians of the passing of their troops over the territory of East Germany in which Berlin is situated. Until now all that was going well. After the declaration that East Berlin is free, the Allies would no longer have to deal with the questions of formalities with the Soviets, but with the East German authorities. America does not want to deal with this little country. To me this seems incompatible with her [America's] honor. In my opinion she [America] should have dealt with the East German authorities. It would have been the simplest way.

But the Soviet would never think of preventing America from keeping troops in Berlin! That doesn't interest them. At present we are seeking a solution for the creation of the free city of Berlin. This would irritate Bonn and Adenauer. The Soviets have nothing against the project of the free city of Berlin. What complicates everything is that we want to treat all the Soviet-American questions together. The question of Berlin and the question of the Secretary General of the UN! And so we get no further.

But there is no danger at all that the Soviets want to go to war over Berlin. And we in Europe are surprised that in the U.S.A. there is talk of going to war because of Berlin and of the question of fighting and, eventually, dying, for Berlin. I do not understand why the diplomats speak of this eventuality. One must be out of one's mind to speak in that fashion.

So, rest easy. One can speak a lot of foolishness in politics, but we have to remember that we can all be wiped out by a bomb in a few minutes. *In public I never discuss the problem of Berlin, because it is stupid. It does not merit the importance it is being given. I give my opinion only on the problem of disarmament and peace!* This is the real problem. And it is there that the people ought to raise their voices!

I am writing you late at night. I do not see why world opinion should be taken up with the problem of Berlin!

Your devoted
Albert Schweitzer

[UNDATED][17]

[undated]

Dear friend,

Here is my opinion about the European situation. However, it is only for you personally. The Berlin crisis is slowly cooling off. It developed because Kennedy, instead of simply negotiating with the Soviets directly, started a mobilization and a tremendous strengthening of the army and sent even more American troops to Berlin, among which were some trained in street-fighting! Even England and France sent more troops to Berlin, and suddenly there was the Berlin airlift and a great panic in East Berlin. Kennedy should have been able to anticipate this.

Now one hears in Europe that Kennedy has to explain his actions to a prowar faction that has developed in the U.S., and that he does so with considerable energy. One also hears that he, unlike his predecessors, will not continue to support Adenauer's policy to let the Berlin question continue to exist with all its inherent danger, instead of solving it. It is assumed that he will agree to Russia's making peace with East Germany and that the Berlin program will not continue to exist in its current form. This peace means that East Berlin will become a free state and that Adenauer and West Berlin must put up with the fact that they won't have any further claims against East Berlin, which is something they dislike very much. But nothing can be done about it, since there is such a "distance" between the two German states, so that East Germany will never agree to be united with West Germany in today's conditions. England as well is for East Germany's independence. However, France, i.e., de Gaulle, stands closer to Adenauer and his policy about Germany. France has increased the number of troops in Germany.

In some German circles it is not considered impossible that Adenauer would attack the freed East Germany to unite it by force with West Germany. It is possible that de Gaulle will help him with this. Whether or not NATO will go along with this plan I don't know. There is a small circle in West Germany who would agree to a war to conquer East Germany.

Certainly each military action of Adenauer would lead to the Soviet entry into the war. And the superiority of the Soviets in Europe would be so strong that Germany and France and NATO would have no chance of success. NATO would have a total value of seventeen divisions (nominally there would be twenty-three divisions). And all other troops would first have to be moved from the west to the theater of war. The Soviets would have forty-five excellently equipped divisions. The French journal *Match* recently printed a very objective article about a war between Germany and NATO versus the Soviets and concluded that the Soviet would remain the absolute winners. There is also the question whether the German parliament would be for a war against East Germany. Therefore, a war-like action on behalf of Adenauer vs. East Germany would be an adventure without a chance of success.

America would probably resist this "adventure." It is questionable whether Adenauer would dare to do this, in spite of his big speeches. Whenever America finally agrees to East Germany's freedom, peace will be maintained and a better state of affairs will be created in Europe than currently exists. This is strictly between us, because I normally do not comment on the Berlin question. I only concern myself with disarmament and peace. The U. S. should have concerned itself with East Germany's independence and the peace treaty between the Soviets and East Germany, instead of letting the unsolved problem of Berlin continue, which is troubling the whole world.

> Thinking of you,
> Sincerely,
> Albert Schweitzer

---

OCTOBER 30, 1961[18]

> Lambaréné, Gabon
> October 30, 1961

Dear friend:

I cannot do as you ask. I did not insist that Khrushchev halt the resumption of tests and I have never publicly denounced him (though in my heart I have denounced him absolutely). I cannot ask Kennedy by telegram not to take up testing in turn. They would say in America that I am meddling as a stranger in trying to influence the president of the United States.

My role is to make appeals to enlighten public opinion in all countries as to the situation in which we find ourselves and to explain what must be done to avoid war and to achieve peace. In attempting to address myself directly to Kennedy, I should do harm to the influence I might have in the U. S. A. The peoples of today are very susceptible to voices coming from abroad.

The resumption of large nuclear tests was in preparation for months in the East and the West. Some members of the American military are demanding that nuclear testing be resumed above ground as well as underground. Since they left off attending the conference for the cessation of nuclear testing at Geneva, the Soviets have been meditating on the resumption of testing, judging that their nuclear arms were not equal to those of the United States. And in America the military set itself the task of calming public opinion by repeating constantly that the Soviets were more advanced in the construction of satellites, but that American nuclear weapons were far superior to the Soviets', or something of that order.

In this situation the resumption of nuclear testing was the temptation to which East and West had to succumb. The Soviets were first to succumb. It was they who shocked the world and who shall bear the consequences in world public opinion. The U. S. A., in resuming tests, can say that the Soviets made it a necessity.

Thus what has happened is what necessarily had to happen. It was inevitable after the breaking off of talks on a test ban. The continuation of the perfecting of weapons necessarily entails the resumption of nuclear tests. These tests are necessary for the creation of arms superior to those in existence.

It is deplorable, it is terrible, it is agonizing. We are sinking ever more deeply into inhumanity by the resumption of tests. For thousands of men are condemned to suffer and to die from nuclear radiation, and generations of newborn children will continue in increasing numbers to be deformed, incapable of living.

All this is happening because public opinion the world

over has treated lightly the dangers of nuclear radiation. It thought that radiation did not hasten the necessity of the renunciation of tests and nuclear weapons. It let the military and the diplomats be, as if it were a question of ordinary politics. . . .

Will public opinion awake to the situation created by this negligence? I have been working for months on the wording of a new appeal! But it is impossible to finish it and to publish it. The situation of nuclear politics never ceases to change. It is never stabilized. Therefore one cannot judge nor advise. The text that I made a month ago no longer corresponds to reality. It is outdated by events. I am watching and when I think I am able to criticize and to propose, I shall speak.

My hope is that, by the gravity of the situation created by the resumption of tests, men throughout the world will understand that they must arrive at a solution to the problem of the terrible danger in which humanity is placed. They can no longer let things go, as they have been doing. We must understand that we are risking the terrible catastrophe in which humanity will perish.

You see, dear friend, how I follow my path, and how I am faithful to you in my work. . . .

So let us struggle.

> With kindest regards,
> your devoted Albert Schweitzer

---

OCTOBER 22, 1962[19]

October 22, 1962

Norman Cousins

Dear friend:

At last I am getting down to replying to your letter of October 1st. You are sad that those who are fighting against nuclear arms may be tiring and may be becoming less enthusiastic than in the first days of the struggle. I have gone through the same experience.

But I think, however, that people are beginning to doubt that there will be a future for nuclear weapons and are realizing their danger. After the events that have taken place, they are beginning to understand that the unlimited production of nuclear weapons can be ruinous to the economy. One can no longer go into the construction of nuclear arms in order to maintain one's supremacy. The economy will no longer permit it. Nuclear weapons are beginning to be a grave problem, one that will continue, year after year, to undermine economies.

People are also beginning to understand that politics between East and West, where one wants to surpass the other, are stupid, and that it is simpler to live side by side in peace. Dear friend: time works for those of us who wish to abolish nuclear weapons. The world will see that nuclear weapons are a burden of which we must relieve ourselves.

And the idea of peace is also on the march. I have taken the trouble to inform myself about the meetings at the congress in Moscow. They are dominated by the conviction that nothing is in the way of peaceful coexistence in the world. We live in a time where the problems of Cuba and Berlin are the only ones under discussion between the East and West. They are, at heart, small problems. That will be realized more and more, as soon as reason takes hold.

So, let us continue our struggle against nuclear arms; let us not be discouraged by the weariness of former companions in the struggle.

Yours devotedly,<br>Albert

P.S. I have at present a proposition to make: In the U. S. it has been decided to use nuclear arms for the questions of Cuba and Berlin. This is a new and serious decision. I should never have thought that the government would dare to take this decision, such a serious one. And I am of the opinion that we must not accept this decision without protesting. *To start the debate, I think it might be useful for me to write an open letter to [Secretary of Defense] McNamara, to whom the United States government has made known that in a conflict over Cuba and in the case of Berlin it might use all its forces,* which would mean nuclear arms as well. I am sending you this open letter, most respectfully in which I am presenting to him the gravity of the government decision with which he is charged. I attempt to explain to him the gravity of the decision and the terrible responsibility that he will have to bear vis-à-vis humanity. I am sending you the text of the letter in German, with the translation by Mademoiselle Ali Silver, the nurse who helps me with English correspondence. You may change the translation if you believe it can be improved.

Can you find an American magazine that would publish this letter? If you find a magazine would you simply wire me "Magazine found" (journal trouvé). Then I will also try to have the letter published in European magazines. I hope that you will be able to publish the letter in several American magazines. Also offer the letter on my behalf to the American-German review *Aufbau* in New York. The editor-in-chief is an old friend of mine.

So I await your telegram. I hope that you are of the same opinion as I. Also send as soon as possible twelve copies (tear sheets?) of the open letter in English. I shall use them for Japan and India and England. We must fight. We will not let nuclear war come so simply into the world today. Let us struggle. I shall also send the English text to Lord Russell.

So I don't forget: Of course I shall be very happy to have you in Lambaréné and for as long as possible! I am delighted at the prospect of having you with us.

Fondly,<br>Albert

P.S. Please telephone Mrs. Erica about the open letter.

---

Dear Mr. McNamara:

I learned from the newspapers that the government of the United States gives you, in your function of Secretary of Defense, the permission to undertake, in the question of Cuba as well as in that of Berlin, everything which you consider necessary. You are also allowed to decide for a war, fought with all kinds of weapons, also atomic weapons, when you judge this necessary.

Your government does you the honor to give you permission to make a decision in this so serious matter.

The fact that the government of the United States in the present situation leaves to somebody the decision about peace or war also caused consternation in the world, as the government makes known herewith that it came to the resolution to leave the decision in the Cuba question and the Berlin question to an atomic war.

This has never been clearly stated before. All over the world an atomic war has been considered as something so exceptional that, because of its horribleness, it could not be earnestly considered and risked.

Where you have been entrusted to decide for an atomic war, does this mean an unexpected, very serious aggravation of the political situation in the world?

A war, fought with atomic weapons, is something so horrible that not even military people, or the scientists, concerned with the real significance of atomic weapons, can have a full notion about it.

First of all, it no longer has the character of a war. War up to now has meant that through the use of weapons territory can be conquered or can be defended against enemies and that through the use of better weapons one can have a superiority which forces the opponent to surrender and to make peace.

A war with atomic weapons is very different. During such a war no territory or fortress can be conquered, no territory or fortress can be defended. The only possibility is mutual, senseless, unlimited destruction. Destruction will take place over vast territories, far over the borders of the combatants, because of explosions, fire, and a terrible poisoning of the atmosphere and soil. A great part of many populations will perish woefully.

Atomic war also has nothing to do with two belligerent nations, but with the whole of humanity. He who decides for an atomic war takes a terrible responsibility toward mankind. Nobody can release him from this responsibility.

Do leave us the hope, dear sir, that you are conscious of the terrible responsibility which would burden you in the case that you should decide to risk an atomic war because of the Cuban or Berlin question.

And, moreover, may you be confident that both of these problems can be much better solved by quiet, positive negotiations which try to maintain peace than by a war. Politics of strength are in our time not the right ones, because they are provocative and poison the atmosphere. I kindly ask you to excuse me, dear sir, because I have decided to write to you about this matter. I cannot do otherwise. I feel compelled to do so because of the great danger in which the human race finds itself.

Yours devotedly,
Albert Schweitzer

---

## OCTOBER 31, 1962[20]

Lambaréné
October 31, 1962

Norman Cousins

Dear friend:

Thank you for your wire. Naturally, we did well not to attack McNamara, given the grave turn of events, which I hadn't been able to foresee. But when peace is established, we must, in our struggle against nuclear weapons, criticize the fact that McNamara did something very grave in announcing that he would use all forces—that is to say nuclear arms as well—in a war over the problem of Cuba or of Berlin. If we are really fighting against nuclear arms, we cannot abstain from criticizing McNamara, severely and publicly. Otherwise, we fail in our duty. We cannot make concessions. Naturally, President Kennedy was in agreement with McNamara. But one doesn't make public attacks on the president.

But McNamara's decision to say that the use of nuclear weapons was a possibility was a world provocation that was stupid and very serious. We must talk very clearly about it when the crisis has passed.

Above all, that he should speak of the Berlin crisis. For me as for others who know the reasons for the Berlin crisis, this is a stupidity about which the Germans must be arguing among themselves. For those who know the problem, to think of an atomic war over Berlin is idiocy. The American secretary of defense ought not to be concerned with that. And if there is an atomic war because of Berlin, the first thing that will happen is that the two Berlins will cease to exist—thanks to the use of atomic weapons. The Berliners know it and are afraid of a war because of it. We Europeans find it strange that the American secretary of defense should take up the Berlin question and offer to the Berliners an atomic war as the solution to the Berlin problem. Berliners would rather stay alive. Forgive me for writing you to say how much the idea of an atomic war to bridge the Berlin problem seems idiotic. All this is entirely between ourselves.

Devotedly,
Albert

---

NOVEMBER 11, 1962[21]

Lambaréné
November 11, 1962

Dear friend:

Thank you for your letter of October 30th. First, the McNamara question. You say that he is on the side of the moderates, and yet he announced coldly, proudly, with Kennedy, that if war should come he would use atomic weapons. Where is the moderate? The moderate acted like an extremist, with unbelievable frivolity, as did President Kennedy. This is something very grave for the world, for one must think also of the world and of humanity, who will have to submit to an atomic war, for an all-out atomic war becomes immediately a world war. And it is necessary to point out to those who declare that they will use atomic weapons their responsibility vis-à-vis the world. I wrote to Lord Russell that I am against making public reproaches to Kennedy, because he is chief of state. A chief of state must be criticized in public only if absolutely necessary. Therefore, one can only criticize McNamara. And as the crisis has passed, I feel that I shall give up the idea of criticizing a military leader of the U.S. I will withdraw the letter to

McNamara, as you suggest. But will you, an American, denounce this frivolity, so that the American military authorities may realize their responsibilities not only to America but also to the world? You know how much I love America. I am profoundly saddened when I hear that the newspapers are talking about a war hysteria brought on by the Cuban crisis. And what would have become of you, and of us with you, if Khrushchev had not put aside all question of prestige and simply offered to surrender. Great peoples haven't the right to abandon themselves to hysteria.

And that McNamara and Kennedy would have declared that they would use atomic weapons as well if the Berlin question gave way to war. The Berlin question is a European one. It can be settled easily if the two Germanys begin to look for a solution. Basically, it is merely a question of formalities. If the U.S. wants to help solve it, the most useful thing would be simply to withdraw its troops from Europe as it promised to do by the Treaty of Potsdam. It is abysmal folly for McNamara and Kennedy to think themselves obliged to fight a nuclear war over Berlin. A nuclear war cannot settle anything. It can only lead to inestimable destruction, as the military must know and must take into consideration. Nuclear war over Berlin means that within the space of one hour Germany will cease to exist.

Forgive me for being a bit strong. But I was terrified to hear that the head of the army and the president of the U.S. deemed it useful to consider a nuclear war not only over the Cuban crisis, which is their business, but as well over the Berlin crisis, which is not and which they do not understand. And in the U.S. everyone accepted this idiotic declaration about a nuclear war waged by the United States to settle the Berlin problem! Where are we going? You, the reasonable people in America, must educate your military and your politicians. The world must return to reason and give up these funny ideas that spring up in the imaginations of military men and politicians. We in Europe and you in America must see to this task. We must create a new state of mind if the danger of a ruinous catastrophe for humanity is to be avoided. So, I shall go to work in Europe with regard to these latest developments and shall give up the idea of criticizing, as a foreigner, American personalities. Things must be kept in order.

I am well, but my work is considerable and unceasing day to day. The amount of my correspondence is crushing me. It gets bigger every year.

With my best wishes, profoundly and devotedly yours,

Albert

P.S. In Germany, the Adenauer regime, anti-democratic as it is, becomes more and more insupportable. It is giving itself over more and more to the militarists.

## Notes

1. Editor and writer Norman Cousins and Dr. Schweitzer corresponded during the final decade of the latter's life, from 1955 to 1965. Most of their correspondence was unpublished until Cousins issued his book, *Albert Schweitzer's Mission: Healing and Peace*. This is a remarkable collection of letters, written from 1957 to 1963, beginning with Cousins' visit to Lambaréné early in 1957. Only those letters, or portions thereof, dealing directly with the issues of this volume are included here.
2. Published in Cousins, *Albert Schweitzer's Mission*, pp. 164–166.
3. *Ibid.*, pp. 174–175.
4. *Ibid.*, pp. 189–190. This letter was written 12 days after the "Declaration of Conscience" was broadcast.
5. *Ibid.*, pp. 198–199. Schweitzer was on one of his infrequent visits to Europe when he wrote this letter from his home in Günsbach. Harold Stassen was special assistant to President Eisenhower on disarmament affairs. Ralph Flanders was a U.S. Senator from Vermont (1946–1959) and took an active role in congressional oversight of the U.S. Atomic Energy Commission.
6. *Ibid.*, pp. 200–201. In this period the National Committee for a Sane Nuclear Policy (SANE) was being organized in the U.S.—with Cousins as Co-Chairman—along with the Campaign for Nuclear Disarmament (CND) in England. It is unlikely that this letter was actually written in Lambaréné, because Schweitzer returned to Africa from Europe for his thirteenth and final sojourn in Africa only in December 1957; see the opening lines of the following letter.

7. *Ibid.,* pp. 202–203. The "appeal to reason" must be the first advertisement which SANE inserted in American newspapers, written by Norman Cousins.
8. *Ibid.,* pp. 208–210.
9. *Ibid.,* pp. 215–217. This letter is in reply to a long letter by Cousins, dated May 9, 1958, in which Cousins asks if it would be useful if an appeal to the World Court were signed "by no more than half a dozen of the world's moral leaders including you and Pope Pius XII."
10. *Ibid.,* pp. 219–221.
11. *Ibid.,* pp. 222–225. The telegram was sent a few days earlier from Norman Cousins informing Schweitzer that the "United States just announced provisional suspension of nuclear testing." Cousins added: "Congratulations. All good wishes to you for the completion of your objective for world peace." Schweitzer sent this letter via Erica Anderson (who was living in the United States) for translation. In an accompanying note to her, Schweitzer asserted: "Now I learn from the clippings of the newspapers that it [the moratorium on U.S. testing] will be only for one year and will not start until the 31st of October. How poverty stricken and full of clauses is this thing! A thinking process in installments!" Neverless, Schweitzer felt that he had to write Cousins this "letter of thanks." He wrote Miss Anderson: "I felt the need to write all this down in the moments of the first triumph, for both of us [Cousins and Schweitzer]." He admitted that "in a few months all the details of this battle may not be as clearly in my head as they are now." (See Cousins, *Albert Schweitzer's Mission,* p. 222.)
12. *Ibid.,* pp. 227–228. "Your friendly writing" was a letter from Cousins dated September 4, 1958.
13. *Ibid.,* pp. 233–236. The "open letter to Geneva" was a message to the disarmament negotiators at Geneva. It originated with Norman Cousins and was published in *The Saturday Review* on November 22, 1958. Schweitzer led the sixteen signatories. Others included Martin Niemoeller, C. Rajagopalachari of India, Toyohiko Kagawa of Japan, Trygve Lie of Norway, Lord Boyd-Orr, Bertrand Russell, Mrs. Eleanor Roosevelt, and Gunnar Myrdal.
14. *Ibid.,* pp. 237–238. This letter is in response to one from Cousins about the latter's project to provide medical care and assistance to Polish women who were victims of Nazi medical experiments. Cousins planned to visit Warsaw and Berlin and

sought Schweitzer's help to seek reparations and compensation from West Germany.

15. *Ibid.,* pp. 241–242.
16. *Ibid.,* pp. 270–271. This letter was in answer to one written by Cousins on October 2, 1961, in which he wrote about a visit with Secretary of State Dean Rusk on the problem of Berlin.
17. *Ibid.,* pp. 272–273.
18. *Ibid.,* pp. 274–276. When the United States announced that it was resuming tests of nuclear weapons in the atmosphere, Cousins cabled Schweitzer, urging that the latter immediately send his objections to President John F. Kennedy. Schweitzer sent a cable to Cousins: "Impossible to do what you ask." This letter was an explanation of the cable.
19. *Ibid.,* pp. 283–287.
20. *Ibid.,* p. 288. After receiving Schweitzer's letter of October 22, 1962, with the draft letter to Secretary of Defense Robert S. McNamara, Cousins cabled Schweitzer: "Holding up your McNamara statement. Turn of events in U.S. may require changes. Letter follows."Cousins wrote to Schweitzer on October 30, 1962 containing"certain facts that may have a bearing" on the open letter to Secretary McNamara. Cousins pointed out that McNamara belonged"to the moderate faction in the government." (Cousins, *Albert Schweitzer's Mission,* p. 287–294).
21. *Ibid.,* pp. 294–296. This is the last letter from Schweitzer published in this series. Cousins cabled Schweitzer on July 21, 1963 that a "nuclear test-ban now imminent" and later wrote to *Schweitzer* on October 4, 1963, that the partial test-ban treaty had been ratified. The letter of October 30, 1962 from Cousins contained "certain facts that may have a bearing" on the open letter to Secretary McNamara. Cousins pointed out that McNamara belonged "to the moderate faction in the government." (Cousins, *Albert Schweitzer's Mission,* pp. 289–294).

# 6

## Letters to Bertrand Russell

*In October 1955, Albert Schweitzer went to London to receive
the Order of Merit from Queen Elizabeth II. While in London,
Schweitzer was given a reception in the restaurant owned by
an old friend from Alsace, Emil Mettler. Philosopher Bertrand
Russell attended this event. Russell and Schweitzer talked
briefly and this encounter led to a correspondence between the
two which extended during the remaining decade of Schweitzer's life.*

*Professor Herbert Spiegelberg, a friend of Schweitzer
originally in Strasburg, collected, annotated, and published
the Schweitzer-Russell correspondence.[1] Not all of Schweitzer's letters are given here and, regretfully because of the
limitation of space, none by Russell.*

---

DECEMBER 31, 1957[2]

Albert Schweitzer
Lambaréné, Gabon
French Equatorial
Africa
December 31, 1957

Mr. Bertrand Russell, London

Dear Sir,

On the last evening of 1957 I find you in my thoughts and

want to tell you how much I appreciate what you have undertaken this year to prepare the road for the idea of peace. I have informed myself about all that you have achieved. I attach much importance to the fact that with the help of your friends in the U. S. A. you were able to organize a meeting of important people from East and West for discussions of the world situation today. Your open letter to Eisenhower and Khrushchev has expressed the thoughts which circulate among those who are preoccupied with the question of our future. Allow me to congratulate you for using your authority in this way. I was in Europe in September, October, and November. I could not dream of coming to England. The work that had to be done during these weeks and also my exhaustion did not allow it. I did not even find the time to pass a few days in Paris as I normally do during my stay in Europe.

I have not forgotten that in 1955 while I was staying in London you took the trouble to come and say hello to me in the restaurant of my good friend Mettler. I was deeply touched by this.

For 1958 I am sending you my best wishes for yourself and all that you undertake to make triumphant the cause of peace.

With my best thoughts,

Your devoted,
Albert Schweitzer

---

SEPTEMBER 2, 1961[3]

Albert Schweitzer
Lambaréné, Gabon
September 2, 1961

Lord Bertrand Russell
Committee of 100
73 Goodwin Street
London N4

Dear Friend:

I keep up to date with all you undertake to protest against atomic weapons. I find that you are absolutely right in organizing the protest marches. They are beginning to move the people.

I just received a letter from Mr. Trevor Hatton asking me in your name to forward to you a text addressed to the governments of East and West suggesting that they no longer speak of war with reference to Berlin. I am in complete agreement with you, but I prefer that you be the one to prepare the text because I am too busy and tired these days to draft this text and I am not very well informed concerning the questions regarding Berlin. It is not easy for me to receive information on this matter since I find myself in Lambaréné without anyone to discuss this question. I think that you will draft this letter much better than I could. Of course I will sign it with the others.

My area of concern is more the question of disarmament and peace. I am with you in your struggle.

On the other hand, I wonder whether I should also sign your declaration on the Holy Loch affair. This is a matter which concerns England primarily. Do you not fear people might take it badly that I, a stranger, would allow myself to sign a text on an English matter? Please decide. The text concerning the Berlin question I can naturally sign. I regret not being able to come to Europe in the fall this year as I had the intention of doing. I had to renounce it because of work I have to do to keep my hospital running smoothly. I had planned also to come to England and I was happy at the idea of seeing you again.

With my good thoughts,

> Your devoted,
> Albert Schweitzer

---

JUNE 27, 1962[4]

> Albert Schweitzer
> Lambaréné, Gabon
> Western Equatorial Africa
> June 27, 1962

The Lord Russell,
Plas Penrhyn
Penrhyn Pendrath
Marioneth, Wales

Dear Friend:

I thank you cordially for your dear letter of June 20, 1962. I do not understand how an English military person can so frivolously talk about pushing the button! And it is well that the world learns about such stupid talk, coming from persons who occupy important positions, so people realize in what kind of situation we find ourselves because of this narrow-minded military spirit.

Your invitation to me to join the demonstration against such recklessness, on 9th September, unfortunately I cannot accept. I cannot come to Europe. Also this year I have to renounce going to Europe because of work.

Like you, I am convinced that the fight against atomic weapons must be pursued internationally. All negotiations regarding the abolition of atomic weapons remain without success because no international public opinion exists which demands this abolition! In all propaganda against atomic weapons which I carry on from Lambaréné in letters, newspaper articles, and appeals, I speak of the necessity of a strong public opinion in the world. You know as well as I do that the big obstacle to forming this public opinion in the West is that governments want to prevent the development of this opinion, and use as a weapon to call those who support this opinion as being suspect of being communists. This defamation is the most horrible weapon all those who are dependent have to fear. Just that much more those who are to some extent independent have to show courage and stand for this public opinion. The parliaments cannot be relied on in this matter. They are completely without an opinion and therefore also completely irresponsible in the matter of this great danger in which the nations find themselves. Yet 15 years ago one could not have imagined such behavior of parliaments. Today it is accepted as something that is part of our time.

Unfortunately, I have no English translation of what I have written in the last months.

We have a steep road ahead of us. Will we still have the time, before the catastrophe which threatens us, to go to the end? Also the newspapers are not conscious of their responsibility. They have no opinion, but behave purely as reporters. When a Japanese newspaper in Tokyo asked me to send them an article concerning the question of atomic weapons, I gave the following title to that text: "Atom Politics Without Public Opinion." How much I would like to see you again! I have a beautiful memory of the visit which you paid me in the restaurant of my friend, Emil Mettler, in London. I am glad that a picture of the dialogue between you and me in that house exists. At that time we did not sense that one day we would have to pull this heavy carriage together.

I hope you will remain with us for a long time, dear friend.

Cordially your devoted,
Albert Schweitzer

By mistake I have written you in German instead of French. Excuse me please.

---

SEPTEMBER 2, 1962[5]

September 2, 1962

The Earl Russell
Plas Penrhyn
Penrhyndendraeth
Merioneth, South Wales

Dear Mr. Russell,

It rains this night for the first time, since the end of May. The dry season will soon be over, a month too early. Dr. Schweitzer has observed these changes in the atmosphere for several days and tries to finish the concrete work for new constructions as soon as possible. Though Dr. Schweitzer has good helpers, he has to supervise and organize from early morning till sunset. Correspondence has to be postponed and this is the reason why Dr. Schweitzer did not reply to your letter of August 10th and why he asked me today to write to you in his name.

Dr. Schweitzer gladly joins with you in an appeal for funds to further the work of the Committee of 100, for which he feels a great sympathy. His thoughts will be with you next Sunday, during the great demonstration at the Air Ministry.

With kindest regards,

> Sincerely yours,
> Miss Ali Silver
> (Dutch nurse)

---

Dear Friend,

I think of you rather often and I admire everything you are undertaking to impress men to bring themselves to protest against atomic weapons. One cannot abolish them because there is no public opinion which demands it. The guarantee which an abolition requires does not exist. Only public will and opinion demanding abolition can give this guarantee. We are still far from this guarantee since everyone who declares himself against atomic weapons in Europe and the U.S.A. is considered an evil person . . . .

I had hoped to come to Europe this year and to meet you again in London. But I had to give up this plan. The work to be done in Lambaréné does not allow me to be absent.

With my good thoughts,

> Your deeply devoted,
> Albert Schweitzer

---

OCTOBER 18, 1962[6]

> Albert Schweitzer
> Lambaréné, Gabon
> West Equatorial Africa
> October 18, 1962

The Earl Russell
Plas Penrhyn
Penrhyndendraeth
Marioneth, U.K.

Dear Friend,

Just now I received your dear letter of the 11th of October

which moved me deeply because I can see how you are suffering because we have not been able to create a public opinion which would demand the cessation of atomic test explosions and the abolition of atomic weapons. The situation is connected with the apathy in which the parliaments and press find themselves. This is why it is so difficult for you and us, your fellow combatants, to bring about a change in public opinion. You believe that, when we have larger financial resources to use for the distribution of our propaganda in press and films, we obtain better results. Therefore, you are planning to establish a large peace foundation which will collect the funds that will be available to us for more effective propaganda. Certainly this can be significant. But I believe that we should not overestimate its value. This great strength in propaganda cannot really overcome the apathy in which the nations find themselves.

Until now we have talked and fought based on the authority of our clear judgment and our recognition of the danger in which humanity finds itself. This has given our struggle some success and your demonstrations, which have the significance of confessions, have been successful in the past and will continue to be so in the future. This is a kind of natural propaganda from one human being to another.

I believe that, when we are successful in establishing a foundation through which we receive larger financial resources, it will be of great help to us. Let us try. But we should not follow a pattern of common mass propaganda which will use all its means for just any result. Our propaganda is passed on from man to man; its strength is that it represents what is true and sensible. Our propaganda has dignity. It works with simple means; it is noble. This we may not abandon and we must not ever adjust to a propaganda which uses any available means. We are prophets of the truth who can save the world. As such we appear, as such we are respected, as such we can have success. We will continue to do that. Duty drives us to do this. We have to keep our courage.

You, dear friend, have no real conception of the effect your demonstrations have in the world! Continue with them! I see the situation considerably better than you do. There are many people today who have doubts about the dominating public opinion, but will not openly admit it. Believe me!

What is happening in the world today proves to the people that we are telling the truth. It is becoming obvious that the stockpiling of atomic weapons will in the end lead to economic ruin! Everyone is beginning to feel this very much and it will be more noticeable in the future . . . And that is where thoughtlessness will stop. Then, people will become receptive to the truth which we are proclaiming.

I have seen this coming. But I did not believe that it would come so soon and so clearly. Therefore, we shall stay courageous and in a simple way continue tirelessly to announce this grim truth.

I also see the atmosphere at the Moscow Congress as progress in the relationship between East and West. People are beginning to be more reasonable than they were before in their judgment of communism. The anti-communism of the Dulles period is beginning to falter.

I think it is important for me that we try to dissuade those states which do not have atomic weapons from believing that the problems of atomic weapons are none of their concern. I have had the experience that magazines and newspapers in those countries are glad to accept articles from us, and are beginning to reflect on the problems of atomic weapons.

I consider it also a valuable achievement that all have to acknowledge that Khrushchev wants peace.

I also believe that we have to continue in a simple way to announce courageously the truth that we have to get rid of atomic weapons. Time is beginning to tell us that we are right. People have no choice but to join us. Affectionately.

Your faithfully devoted,<br>Albert Schweitzer

This letter is for you personally. I do not want it to be printed, but if you want to share the contents with one or the other of our fellow combatants, I will not object.

OCTOBER 24, 1962[7]

Albert Schweitzer
Lambaréné, Gabon
West Equatorial Africa
October 24, 1962

Lord Bertrand Russell
Plas Penrhyn

Dear Friend:

There is something new in the subject of atomic weapons. You might have noticed that yourself. McNamara, the minister of defense of the U. S. A., and Kennedy are publicly declaring that should it come to hostilities about the Cuban situation or the Berlin situation, all kinds of weapons, including atomic weapons, would be used.

This is a big deterioration in the area regarding [the] problems of atomic weapons. Those two make light of anything that concerns atomic weapons. Until now, the employment of atomic weapons has been considered a problem and has been treated as such. There have been negotiations about the abolition of atomic weapons and these negotiations are still going on. We assume that while these negotiations are taking place, no civilized country would decide to use atomic weapons. Now the U. S. A. takes this step! That means the whole situation has deteriorated, has really deteriorated.

The U. S. is taking part in these negotiations and considers it, unbelievably, its right simultaneously to use atomic weapons.

Therefore, these negotiations about atomic weapons are losing their meaning. They have no longer any significance if America will actually use atomic weapons. And these negotiations have also made progress even if they have not reached their goal. The atmosphere has indeed improved. That can be seen by the course that this international congress on general disarmament and peace in the summer in Moscow has taken. There ruled a fine spirit.

This has meaning for future negotiations of politicians. They have to try harder and they have to be willing to meet half way. I believe we will be successful if we still have enough time.

And McNamara and Kennedy should destroy this perspective for us by their utilization of atomic weapons? Is the U.S.A. really in agreement with their intentions? Does public opinion in America go along with them? I find that we in the world (outside) have to rebel against this. In the press and in assemblies we have to protest. These two in America must know that we will not yield! The matter is very serious! We have to act.

Let me know whether you share this opinion and are ready to speak up. It seems to me absolutely necessary to do so.

> Cordially, yours faithfully,
> Albert Schweitzer

---

## NOVEMBER 11, 1962[8]

> Lambaréné
> November 11, 1962

Dear Friend:

I am enclosing a letter, which I have written to you on 14th October, to tell you that we have to criticize vehemently the recklessness of Kennedy and McNamara who announced that they would be prepared to use atomic weapons in the Berlin and Cuban crises. Since the crisis has now passed, I did not send the letter. During the crisis I was not worried for a moment. I knew that Khrushchev is not concerned with prestige, as is Kennedy and others, and could [also] make concessions if it should be necessary to keep the peace. And this is what actually happened. Kennedy has to be grateful to him for this, for the rest of his life, since Khrushchev saved him from the terrible situation he had gotten into because of his policy of strength. Nations cannot help [otherwise] but listen attentively in astonishment as to how he saved the peace in such a simple way. And now we may hope that we can abolish atomic weapons and attain peace.

Since the situation is now better, we should call McNamara to account and have him tell us how he dared to declare that if there were hostilities arising on account of the Berlin and Cuban crises, atomic weapons would be used. Both questions are only soluble through rational negotiations. I am thoroughly familiar with the Berlin question. This situation seems so difficult because Adenauer does not want to recognize the German Democratic Republic. I suppose he will have to come around to it. It has dire consequences that the U.S.A., England, and France agreed that [West] Germany, which had given its promise in the Potsdam Agreement not to rearm, broke its commitment and started to rearm. They did not think Germany would become a big military power and one day demand atomic weapons. . . .

With regard to the folly of the announcement that atomic weapons would be used in the war with Cuba, I suggest that we only attack and condemn McNamara who is the military commander and do not mention Kennedy because he is the head of state. People do not tolerate it lightly when their head of state is criticized. I would hope that we agree on this. Kennedy will be pleased if he is not mentioned. He will be penitent when he is spared the humiliation of a public judgment.

With my best thoughts.

Yours faithfully,
Albert Schweitzer

---

JANUARY 12, 1965[9]

Lambaréné
January 12, 1965
Republic of Gabon

Mr. Bertrand Russell
Plas Penrhyn
Penrhyn Dendraeth
Marioneth, Wales

Dear Friend,

I thank you for your dear wishes for my ninetieth birthday. We both have the luck at this age still to be able to work. On my birthday I have had the joy to see so many friends from Europe in Lambaréné. Unfortunately, the hospital is still getting larger, much larger than I had planned. Each year one or two new buildings for the sick have to be added to those already in existence. Luckily, I have learned how to build and can supervise the building myself. The trees of the jungle provide us with wonderfully hard wood for the buildings.

Naturally I am also here occupied with the great problems of peace and atomic weapons. Through Einstein I came to occupy myself with the problems of atomic weapons. We have been friends since youth.

How things are standing today I cannot really judge. I hope that your Peace Foundation is helping to create a new spirit in the world.

I do not believe that de Gaulle and West Germany can possibly bring the world into a war with atomic weapons. That the U.S.A. and the Soviet Union walk together is very fortunate. . . .

Unfortunately, it does not look that I will come once more to Europe and we will see each other again. In the year 1959 I was in Europe the last time. The big work to be done here does not allow me to travel. With my best thoughts,

Your cordially devoted friend,
Albert Schweitzer

P.S. I thank you cordially for the friendly lines which you wrote about me for the program of the Esterhazy Orchestra which gave a concert for my birthday.[10]

---

## Notes

1. Herbert Spiegelberg of Washington University in St. Louis, Missouri, reconstructed the correspondence between Bertrand Russell and Albert Schweitzer in a 45-page article published in *International Studies in Philosophy,* vol. 12 (1980). He traced 42 letters, including 17 by Schweitzer. Of these, eight are pertinent to this collection.

   Albert Einstein, in a letter to Russell dated March 4, 1955, suggested to him that "it would be highly desirable to have

Albert Schweitzer join our group" since "his moral influence is very great and worldwide." (*Einstein on Peace*, ed. by Otto Nathan and Heinz Norden, New York: Simon & Schuster, 1960, p. 630). The correspondence between Einstein and Russell resulted in the "group" signing the Einstein-Russell Manifesto against nuclear weapons. This was released on July 9, 1955, before Schweitzer and Russell met on October 20th that year.

2. Published in Spiegelberg (1980). This letter, written in French, is the seventh in an exchange which began with a letter from Schweitzer in October or November 1955 (the letter is undated). This letter refers to Russell's efforts for peace during 1957, especially the organization of the first Pugwash Conference of Scientists from both East and West. It also reflects Russell's letters that year to both President Eisenhower and Secretary Khrushchev reminding both that "what they and their two countries had in common was far more important than their differences."

3. *Ibid.* Translated from the French. At the time Russell was head of the Committee of 100, a British peace organization. Trevor Hatton, a member of the Committee, sent Schweitzer a letter (a copy of which apparently no longer exists) on Russell's behalf. The Berlin wall was erected August 13, several weeks before this letter was written.

4. *Ibid.* Translated from the German. Russell's letter of June 10, 1962 (reprinted in Spiegelberg's article) invites Schweitzer to participate in a "great demonstration" the Committee of 100 was holding at the Air Ministry in Whitehall on September 9, 1962. Schweitzer never returned to Europe from Africa after 1959 and Russell himself was absent from the demonstration, but it was held for two weeks.

5. *Ibid.* The first part was written in English and signed by Ali Silver, an associate of Schweitzer and a nurse at the hospital who helped with English correspondence. The second part was written in French. The letter is in answer to one by Russell (given in Spiegelberg's article) dated August 10, 1962 in which the latter asked Schweitzer to "consider joining me in an appeal for funds, the purpose of which is to further the work of the Committee of 100 in this country."

6. *Ibid.* The letter, written in German, is in answer to one, (given in Spiegelberg's article) in which Russell announces that he has been persuaded to establish the Bertrand Russell Peace Foun-

dation and asked Schweitzer to become a sponsor. Russell wanted also to know the thoughts of Schweitzer on "the entire undertaking."

7. *Ibid.* Translated from the German. Spiegelberg was not able to trace the source for Schweitzer's comment that McNamara and President Kennedy had publicly announced they would use atomic weapons in the conflict over Berlin and Cuba if war broke out.

8. Translated from the German.

9. Translated from German. This is the last letter known to be written by Schweitzer to Russell.

10. Russell wrote: "Albert Schweitzer is one of the few who have devoted their lives to the service of man. The range of his achievements and the importance of his personal example mark him as a leader of our time who will be remembered. Dr. Schweitzer's warnings about the dangers of nuclear preparations and the readiness to engage in wars of annihilation are a great service. It is a pleasure to greet this noble young man on the occasion of his ninetieth birthday." Schweitzer also wrote to Russell on the latter's ninetieth birthday: "The world needs stubborn thinkers to awaken it to the havoc of atomic weapons. Einstein was the first to come forward. By the time he was about to depart this life, he knew that others would carry on the resistance. As the most important and daring of these stubborn ones you, dear friend, came forward to bring the fight into motion. You have been given the capacity to make people bold and to pull them along with you. Through you the fight against atomic weapons has been taken further in England than in any other land. You can be sure that this has importance in every country where there is a resistance to these weapons." (Spiegelberg, epilogue.)

# 7

# Other Letters[1]

*Albert Schweitzer had a wide circle of friends and correspondents during his long life. To date his correspondence— abridged or unabridged—has not been published although professor H.W. Bähr of Tübingen University in* Albert Schweitzer An International Bibliography *does list a number of letters which have been individually published, in whole or in part. The letters given in this chapter represent but a tiny sample of the whole Schweitzer correspondence even on nuclear politics. Acknowledgement is made to those who have given permission for these letters to be included in this volume.*

PRESIDENT DWIGHT D. EISENHOWER[2]

Lambaréné
January 10, 1957

The Hon. Dwight D. Eisenhower
The White House
Washington, D.C.

Dear Mr. President:

I send you my heartfelt thanks for your friendly letter in which you send me your good wishes and those of Mrs. Eisenhower on the occasion of my eighty-second birthday. This expression of your good wishes was the first birthday greeting I received. Your generous and kind thoughts touch me deeply.

In my heart I carry the hope I may somehow be able to contribute to the peace of the world. This I know has always been your own deepest wish. We both share the conviction that humanity must find a way to control the weapons which now menace the very existence of life on earth. May it be given to us both to see the day when the world's peoples will realize that the fate of all humanity is now at stake, and that it is urgently necessary to make the bold decisions that can deal adequately with the agonizing situation in which the world now finds itself. . . .

I was very happy to have Mr. Cousins, who will take this letter to you, here with me in Lambaréné. It was rewarding to spend time together and to see how many ideas and opinions we shared.

With assurance of my highest esteem, I am,

Yours devotedly,
Albert Schweitzer

---

PABLO CASALS[3]

November 22, 1958

To: Pablo Casals

Dearest friend,

Thank you for your moving letter. Your speech is notable. Never would I have imagined that you would become advocate and orator of this cause. They wanted to keep a barrier up by which you would not talk, only about peace in general—as if there did not exist the problem of atomic peace! It is a miracle that they let you pronounce the word "atomic" at all. And the good people don't even know what it is about! There exists the great danger that the pro-atomic governments may give the impression that they search for the same thing as we do, when fundamentally they pursue nothing but to sabotage all that precisely can be done for peace in our day. But, after all, the miracle has been produced, and they let you talk with clarity. And they allowed you to pronounce my name.

It has touched me deeply that you have quoted me. But

you ran the risk of not being authorized to declare the argument that atomic weapons are against international law. It is this very argument which has been suppressed so far.

The jurists, in common secret accord, have not occupied themselves with this question in order not to be obliged to give evidence as to the illegality regarding international law, which they say is the duty of governments, according to the constitutions of their countries. I, on my part, have been able to raise the coward's mask, because I had the privilege, as winner of the Nobel Peace Prize, to speak with absolute liberty about all questions pertaining to world peace, via Radio Oslo (because the Nobel Prize is given in Oslo), particularly about the fact that, because atomic weapons are a violation of international law, this means a threat to the continuation of such armament. Therefore the irrefutable legal adherence starts to become recognizable and will become a matter of serious discussion. Never, in our earlier meetings in Europe, would we have imagined that one day we would together descend in the world arena to fight against those who constitute the greatest danger for mankind of the whole world. Thank you, dearest friend!

With my most loving thoughts for your wife and for you, your devoted

A. S.

P.S. Isn't it curious that Switzerland, well-known soil of hospitality to liberties and generosities, should play such a perplexing role in the great discussion!

---

PRESIDENT JOHN F. KENNEDY[4]

Dr. Albert Schweitzer
Lambaréné,
April 20, 1962

Dear President Kennedy,

Would you have the great kindness to forgive me, old as I am, for taking the courage to write to you about the tests, which the United States, together with England, want to carry out when Russia does not accede to your request that an international inspection on their territory takes care that no tests will take place.

I take the courage to write to you about this as someone who has occupied himself for a long time with the problem of atomic weapons and with the problem of peace.

I believe that I may assure you that, with the newest scientific inventions, each test carried out by the Soviet can be detected at a distance by highly developed instruments, which your country possesses and which protect the United States.

I also take the courage, as an absolutely neutral person, to admit that I am not quite convinced that the claim that one state can oblige the other to tolerate an international control commission on its territory is juridically motivated. This right can only exist after the states agree on disarmament. Then a new situation will have been established, which will put an end to the cold war and which will give each state the right to know, through international inspection on each other's territory, that each country meets its obligations to disarm according to the agreement. The same international control will see to it that no test can be carried out.

An urgent necessity for the world is that the atomic powers agree as soon as possible on disarmament under effective international control. The possibility of such disarmament negotiations should not be made questionable by unnecessary appeals for international verification of the discontinuance of testing.

Only when the states agree not to carry out tests any more can promising negotiations about disarmament and peace take place. Also, when this cannot be achieved, the world is in a hopeless and very dangerous state.

I take the courage to draw your attention also to something that concerns you personally. The terrible discovery has been made, as you surely know, that the children of parents who were exposed to radioactive radiation, even a slight one, are normal in the first and the second generations, but from the third and the fourth generations on horrible deformities occur. The children born then are in danger of having deformed feet, hands, and organs, of being blind or of having deformed brains.

These sad happenings are caused by the great sensitiveness of the cells of the reproductive organs to small doses of radioactive radiation. The effect of this radiation is hereditary *and increasing*. From the third and fourth generations on the children are no longer normal but deformed. People do not like to talk about these facts and prefer not to give any importance to them. But nobody can declare it nonexistent.

It is possible that the tests carried out in these times give less fallout than those made before. But this smaller amount of fallout will still cause men and women of our generation to receive radiation through radioactive milk, radioactive vegetables, radioactive water, or in any other way. The smallest doses of radiation on the so sensitive cells of the reproductive organs are sufficient to cause future misery in the third and fourth generations.

It depends on you, dear President, if this horrible misery of future human beings will be realized, when new atomic tests will be carried out. You are, by the position which you have in the present world, the personality who will be burdened with this responsibility.

Please, do consider, if you will take this responsibility by insisting on not absolutely necessary conditions for the cessation of atomic tests or if this terrible responsibility will move you to let the time come in which tests belong to the past and in which promising negotiations about disarmament and peace are at last possible.

It was not easy for me to draw your attention to the great responsibility you hold to protect future generations. Please, forgive me; I could not do otherwise, not only for the sake of humanity, but also out of consideration for you personally.

Yours devotedly,<br>Albert Schweitzer

---

*President Kennedy's Reply*[5]

June 6, 1962

Dear Dr. Schweitzer:

I read your letter on the nuclear testing problem with interest and sympathy. I can assure you that no decision I have taken in my Administration has given me more concern and sorrow than the decision to resume nuclear testing. It was a tragic choice; and I made it only because the alternative seemed to me to offer even greater dangers to or hopes for world peace, to unborn generations to come, and to the future of humanity.

If I had any assurance that the Soviet Union would not test again, I would never have directed that our tests be resumed. But it is impossible to believe that our refusal to test would have deterred the Soviet Union from initiation of a new test series whenever it suited their plans. The Soviet leaders have shown their contempt for world opinion in the past, and deference to this opinion is not likely to constrain them in the future. If the Soviet Union had been able to launch a new series without intervening tests on our part, it is conceivable that a grave shift in the world balance of power might have resulted, with fateful consequences for all our hopes for peace and freedom.

From the start of my Administration, I have tried to negotiate an agreement with the Soviet Union outlawing all nuclear tests. As you know, the Soviet Union has shown little interest in having such an agreement. Until the Soviet Union accepts a meaningful test-ban agreement, I can see no choice, as the man responsible for the future of my country and my people, but to take necessary steps to protect the security position of the United States.

You raise the question of the need for international inspection. At present, national systems are able to detect seismic shocks but not reliably to identify them—i.e., they are not reliably able to distinguish an explosion from an earthquake. Until detection methods improve, there can be no alternative to some limited form of on-site inspection. Obviously such inspection would apply to the United States and Great Britain as well as to the Soviet Union.

I need hardly say that, as the father of two children, I share your concern over the pernicious effect of radioactivity. I can only say that I had to weigh this against the alternative— that is, unlimited testing by the Soviet Union alone, leading to a steady increase in Soviet nuclear strength until the Communist

world could be ready for a final offensive against the democracies. I believe that the Soviet leadership includes men
genuinely devoted to the cause of peace. Our strength reinfor-
ces them in their arguments with their extremist colleagues. It
would seriously undermine their position if their country were
permitted to acquire decisive nuclear superiority.

Nothing lies closer to my heart than the hope of bringing
about general and complete disarmament under conditions of
reliable international control. You are one of the transcendent
moral influences of our century. I earnestly hope that you will
consider throwing the great weight of that influence behind the
movement for general and complete disarmament. I am happy
to attach an outline of the basic provisions for such a treaty. I
also enclose a study by our Arms Control and Disarmament
Agency on "The Detection and Identification of Underground
Nuclear Explosions" and a copy of my speech of March 2 set-
ting forth the considerations which led me to conclude in favor
of the resumption of testing.

Sincerely,<br>John F. Kennedy

---

## TO PRESIDENT JOHN F. KENNEDY[6]

Lambaréné<br>[undated]

Dear Mr. President,

I am writing to congratulate you and to thank you for having had the foresight and the courage to inaugurate a world
policy toward peace. Finally a ray of light appears in the darkness in which humanity was seeking its way and gives us the
hope that the darkness will make way for light.

The treaty between the East and the West to renounce
nuclear tests in the atmosphere and underwater is one of the
greatest events, perhaps the greatest, in the history of the
world. It gives us the hope that war with atomic weapons between East and West can be avoided.

When hearing of the Moscow treaty I thought of my friend,

Einstein, with whom I joined in the fight against atomic weapons. He died in Princeton in despair. And I, thanks to your foresight and courage, am able to observe that the world has taken the first step on the road to peace.

Please accept, Mr. President, the assurance of my highest consideration.

Devotedly,
Albert Schweitzer

---

TO ALBERT EINSTEIN[7]

February 20, 1955

. . . Even without writing we are united in thought, because we experience our terrible times together and in the same way, and we worry together about the future of mankind. When we met in Berlin we could never have imagined that we should be united by such a bond. It is strange how often our names are linked in public. It delights me that we have the same first name. . . .

About the question of new tests with the most modern atomic bomb, I cannot understand that the UN cannot make up its mind to bring the matter to a discussion. I am getting letters asking that you and I and some others should raise our voices to demand such an action of the UN. But we have raised our voices enough. We cannot dictate anything to the UN. It is an autonomous body and has to find in itself the incentive and feeling of responsibility to try to prevent a threatening disaster. From the distance I cannot judge what prevents them to rise to the occasion. And if the attempt proved fruitless it would at least have been undertaken and it would have revealed where the opposition is.

I spent some time in Europe during the second part of 1954. My principal task was to work out the speech for Oslo on the problem of peace. As I had therefore to occupy myself with the history of the thought for peace, I made the, to me, surprising discovery that Kant in his writing "Towards Eternal Peace" is concerned only about the legal side of the problem and not with its ethical side. The ethical side stands in the foreground by Erasmus of Rotterdam. The more one occupies oneself with Erasmus, the more one likes him in spite of his faults. He certainly is one of the most important champions for culture which is built on the humanitarian idea. . . .

---

## TO THE DAILY HERALD[8]

April 11, 1954

IN THE life I lead at Lambaréné, I get so tired and I have so much work to do that I cannot keep up my correspondence as much as I should wish, nor can I find time to write on subjects about which my advice is asked.

It is quite impossible for me to write an 800-word article for you. I am obliged to summon my last reserves of energy in order to carry out the essential work I must do each day.

I cannot even take a normal night's sleep and it is almost midnight as I write these lines to you. Please excuse my delay in replying to you.

I am, however, most anxious to give my views to you personally.

The problem of the effects of H-bomb explosions is terribly disturbing, but I do not think that a conference of scientists is what is needed to deal with it. There are too many conferences in the world today and too many decisions taken by them.

What the world should do is to listen to the warnings of individual scientists who understand this terrible problem. That is what would impress people and give them understanding and make them realize the danger in which we find ourselves.

Just look at the influence Einstein has, because of the anguish he shows in face of the atomic bomb.

It must be the scientists, who comprehend thoroughly all the issues and the dangers involved, who speak to the world, as many as possible of them all telling humanity the truth in speeches and articles.

If they all raised their voices, each one feeling himself impelled to tell the terrible truth, they would be listened to, for then humanity would understand that the issues were grave.

If you and Alexander Haddow [the professor who has pleaded for a United Nations conference of scientists on the H-bomb] can manage to persuade them to put before mankind the thoughts by which they themselves are obsessed, then there will be some hope of stopping these horrible explosions and of bringing pressure to bear on the men who govern.

But the scientists must speak up. Only they have the authority to state that we can no longer take on ourselves the responsibility for these experiments, only they can say it.

There you have my opinion. I give it to you with anguish in my heart, anguish which holds me from day to day.

With my best wishes and in the hope that those who must advise us will make themselves heard.

---

ADLAI E. STEVENSON[9]

> Günsbach,
> Haut-Rhin, France
> [written at Basel,
> November 15, 1957]

Dear Friend:

Clara [Urquhart] tells me that a word from me would give you pleasure in these tormented days through which we are living. I have thought much of you and your cares through all this time. I do not understand why the Western Front has not decided to discuss, in a committee representing a great number of peoples, the proposal of the Eastern Front for stopping nuclear tests. That is the first step to take and the first decision to make if our world is to escape from the anguished situation in which it finds itself.

I do not understand why, instead of seeking to achieve this first result, the Western Front should decide to intensify its nuclear armaments and should wish to furnish these armaments to all the peoples who are allied with it. This is a dangerous enterprise from all points of view. And why clumsy and ill-natured remarks have been pronounced by members of the Government and the Army! One wonders what good that can do. It does no good to the cause of peace, with which we ought to be occupied.

People in Europe are surprised at this attitude of the U. S. A., caused by a little artificial moon turning around our poor earth. They cannot believe this is really the policy of the American people and they hope that voices will be raised in the United States against this noisy policy, caused by the nervousness that the little moon has created. I await with anxiety the Paris meeting. I do not believe it would be to your advantage to associate yourself, even if only formally, with what will be worked out at that meeting. They want your agreement, even in such a qualified form as you might give it. They want you to be there. It will be interpreted as an agreement on your part, even if it is not.

The world must know that the American nation does not consent to this policy, which operates by means of demonstrations and threats which are really not in the interest of the cause of peace. When the French government and the English government declare their adherence to the policy of America, they do not have their peoples behind them. And in Germany these last days, a large part of the nation has declared itself against accepting nuclear arms. The government has announced that it would continue to refuse nuclear arms for its army.

But the essential thing, if the American policy of pushing on with nuclear armaments is not to create a situation from which there will be no escape, is that persons *in* the U. S. A. must have the courage to speak out against it; or, if their situation does not permit that, they must stand aside and avoid anything which would be interpreted as agreement with that policy. If you stand aside, that will be of great importance. Then the press, too, will dare to speak freely. Everything at this moment depends on whether or not in the U. S. A. a point of view contrary to that of the government will make itself felt. If it arises there, it will arise in Europe as well. If not, there is danger that it will be stifled in Europe, too.

As to what I may be able to do in Europe, I say nothing to anyone. I shall act according to circumstances. The signal for non-adherence to the noisy policy of the Western Front should be given in the U. S. A. How sad it is that the press is so apathetic and contents itself with publishing telegrams, instead of presenting an opinion. But let us not despair.

From the heart,
Your devoted,
Albert Schweitzer

---

Lambaréné[10]
December 21, 1959

Dear Adlai Stevenson,

I am happy to have the occasion to write to you. Everything you say and do interests me. If ever you have an oppor tunity to come to Lambaréné for a rest, come. I will be happy to receive you and to talk with you. I am uneasy about the situation of the world. Peace is sought only with banalities. But basically there is no desire to do anything to try to prepare for its coming. NATO continues to encircle the Soviets with medium and also long-distance missile stations. There is talk of resuming the nuclear tests, and the press and public opinion accept this tendency without protest. A meeting is held in preparation for the summit conference, not to seek for a basis of negotiation, but solely to engage mutually to remain together on the old positions, which cannot lead to any agreement.

And these journeys of Chiefs of State! What good are they? To fool the public and make it believe they are seeking peace. You did well to criticize in an article this curious fashion of simultaneous journeys of Chiefs of State.

And what is most serious is that Germany now produces nuclear arms, which the Soviets can never accept, for the decisions of the Potsdam Conference are legally still in effect. They proscribe the rearmament of Germany. The Soviet protests which were made public in recent days are proof of it. This is the great cloud on the horizon to which no attention is paid. The press takes no notice. It wants to ignore it. Public opinion pays no attention. But this cloud that they want to ignore exists and is growing larger. It is the great question of today's political situation. The Soviets will never permit that missile installations be established on German territory and directed against them! For this is the most dangerous region of the encirclement. Where are we going? I write you these lines, because I know that fundamentally you judge the situation as I do.

Please consider this letter as entirely personal and confidential. I think it is useful for you to know my opinion. And if you have the goodness to let me know your own, that will be important for me. What really is the opinion of the public in the U. S. A.? To what extent is it aware of the truth, and what attitudes does it take? I have the impression that it wishes to minimize and ignore as much as possible that which might trouble it.

Naturally, I on my part will treat your letter as entirely confidential.

From the heart
your devoted
Albert Schweitzer

Don't forget that you are invited to spend a weekend at Lambaréné.[10]

---

Lambaréné[11]
June 7, 1960

Dear Friend,

Forgive me that I, egotistically and stupidly, suggested to you that you could now come to see me in Lambaréné! Your place is now in the U. S. to let reason speak and to avoid that politics proceed on the wrong track. Your influence is of great meaning. I am informed currently of what you do and what you say. You yourself will decide whether you will run for the candidate of the presidency or if you consider it better to remain a free politician who, with great influence, can use this influence. In any case it is now your task to be active in politics. I follow your activities through the newspaper clippings and I wish you the best of luck.

What concerns me, I gather through notes for one or two radio appeals. But I believe I will hold them only for the right time. I do not judge pessimistically about the present situation. The main thing will be that Khrushchev and the American President have good relations with each other. Then the sky will look lighter again. Do not inform anyone of this letter.

Devotedly yours,
Albert Schweitzer

---

Lambaréné[12]
July 5, 1960

Dear Friend:

These lines here only tell you that I follow everything which concerns you with great interest. If I understand correctly, you have decided to let yourself be drafted to be a presidential candidate. I believe that what happened with Japan will be favorable for your position because it now becomes so clear to everyone that America's foreign policy is on a wrong road. How could those around the President agree to his plan to visit Japan, in spite of the big demonstrations against the military pact and the hostile atmosphere against his visit? The foreign political situation, through this, has worsened considerably.

[This has occurred because of] the military speeches about the Philippines as well as the Garcia-Eisenhower explanations regarding the question of the security of the Philippines and the necessity for them to be equipped with the "most modern weapons," which means atomic weapons. And then the trip from the Philippines South accompanied with naval ships and an air force! If the President, even in times of peace, can only travel under such powerful cover, then something must be very wrong with the policy.

And to visit Okinawa in the present mood, that is a provocation which one should have saved the President from enduring—and also saved the prestige of America. Everything points to the fact that the course of American foreign policy has to take a different turn, fundamentally so. For such change, you would be the best personality to depend upon. The tremendous expenditures in armament also speak for the necessity to change the present trend. The U. S. cannot continue to spend so much for a long time.

All of this has to be explained to the U. S. people, calmly and gently so that they, almost as if by themselves, begin to understand the whole situation. The facts speak a powerful language. Therefore, the words can be mild.

As for me, I believe that you have at times spoken too sharply. This is my personal opinion. I wonder whether this might not cost you some of the sympathies of the people. You now have to appear the completely level-headed, calm, controlled, superior politician (who you are) and the people will know, by themselves, that you are the right man who, on this stormy voyage, can take the wheel into his hands.

In this difficult situation, people—above all else, and before anything else, will search for the calm-controlled man, of whom the population senses, that he does not aspire for his own big position, but only aspires to fulfill his duty and obligation.

From far away, I wish you courage and luck for that which lies ahead of you, which you have to do.

> With best thoughts,
> Yours devotedly,
> Albert Schweitzer

---

> Lambaréné[13]
> December 27, 1962

Dear Friend:

Your letter gave me great joy. I often think of you and your difficult post and all the work you have to do.

It was a great joy to me to learn that, in the Cuban crisis, you were the only one in the Administration who said: first negotiate! You took the right course. McNamara and Kennedy committed a great mistake when they announced that, in the Cuban problem, as in the Berlin problem, if it came to hostilities, they would instantly use atomic weapons.

They should not have said that. They should not take on themselves this responsibility, especially since they must know that Khrushchev has more than once publicly stated that he would never be the first to use atomic weapons.

It is a grave matter to know that one is responsible for being willing to use atomic weapons. And Kennedy must know this. The world may require him to be conscious of it. It is strange that not a single newspaper in the U. S. A. drew attention to the fact that he announced he would instantly use atomic weapons. And why promise further that he would likewise make instant use of atomic weapons in the Berlin matter? Berlin lies in Europe, and we Europeans do not agree to Kennedy's starting an atomic war in Europe. This speech of Kennedy made a bad impression in Europe. Not Kennedy, but we ourselves, as free men, decide our fate.

And what point would there be in an atomic war over Berlin? The Berlin question is a question of forms. Kennedy must know that. And it cannot be solved with atomic weapons. One hour after the start of an atomic war over Berlin, Berlin will have ceased to exist, and the few survivors will be fleeing to the Rhine.

No political question can be solved by an atomic war. Nowadays even heads of state and generals must know that.

I am constantly occupied with the problem of atomic weapons. That is my fate. The respect that is shown to me by the world must be employed to convince mankind that atomic war is inhuman. When Einstein died, it was a consolation to him that I would carry on the fight against atomic weapons in his spirit. We had become friends before there were any atomic weapons. Our acquaintance dated from the time when he was teaching at the University of Berlin and I was teaching at the University of Strasburg. We saw each other often. The last time was when he was living in England as a refugee . . .

> With warm thoughts,
> Your devoted,
> Albert Schweitzer

JEAN LASSERRE[14]

Lambaréné
February 27, 1965

Dear M. Lasserre,

I accept with pleasure your invitation to become an Honorary member of the Board of Directors of the M.I.R. [Mouvement International de la Réconciliation, a branch of the International Fellowship of Reconciliation]. Heartfelt thanks.

I am still fighting, and have always fought against atomic arms. The situation is not favorable. China has the bomb; other countries, especially in Asia and in Africa, are seeking to get themselves atomic weapons. The Americans may be tempted to use theirs to put an end to the war against the Vietcong...?

With my best wishes,
Faithfully yours,
Albert Schweitzer

P.S. Please excuse the bad handwriting. For a long time I have suffered from writer's cramp. Writing demands a great effort.

---

## Notes

1. Schweitzer wrote many other letters on peace and atomic issues which are not printed in this volume. *See* the new book, *Albert Schweitzer, Lehen, Werk und Denken 1905-1965 Mitgeteilt in seinen Briefen,* ed. by Hans Walter Bähr. Heidelberg: Lambert Schneider. 475 pp. 1987.
2. Published in Cousins, 1985, p. 123.
3. Published in Cousins, 1985, pp. 231-232. Born in Spain in 1876, this eminent cellist, conductor, and humanist died in 1973.
4. Published in Cousins, 1985, pp. 277-279. Schweitzer apparently wrote a later letter to President Kennedy—on November 23, 1962. A copy is found in the Schweitzer archives at Günsbach, France, but it may never have been sent to the President.
5. Published in Cousins, 1985, pp. 279-281.
6. Written probably in August or September 1963. The text is from

Archives centrales Albert Schweitzer in Günsbach, France.
7. Published in Brabazon, pp. 423–424 and in *Schweitzer: A Biography,* by George Marshall and David Poling. New York: Doubleday. 1971. 342 pp., p. 240. Schweitzer wrote this letter after reading the tribute that Einstein paid him in the eightieth birthday *Festschrift* compiled by this editor (Jack, 1955). Einstein died several weeks after receiving this letter—on April 18, 1955. On June 18, 1955, Schweitzer wrote the following letter to Einstein's niece: "The death of your honored uncle has moved me deeply. We got to know each other at a time in Berlin and felt right away drawn to each other. At first it was difficult for me to overcome the shyness which the great physicist inspired. Later on we met at Oxford. We did not get together very often. Also, we did not write to each other frequently. But we both knew that we understood each other and that we had the same ideals. We took part, from a distance, in each other's life. There existed an inner bond between us. We always knew of each other and we heard from each other through other people. I was deeply moved that your uncle had, in writing and in speaking, mentioned me so kindly and that he stressed the similarity of our lives and our conception of the world. . . . It is noteworthy that in the memoria which have been dedicated to him there was mentioned not only the great scholar, but the man and his humanity. He had obviously also as a man his significance in our time, as a representative of a deep humanitarian culture, in a time when it is most important to preserve this ideal for mankind. I consider the friendship with your uncle one of the most beautiful things in my life." (Marshall and Poling, pp. 240–241.)
8. In the spring of 1954, there was world-wide controversy about building the hydrogen bomb. Professor Alexander Haddow proposed that the UN convene a conference of scientists to determine whether the hydrogen bomb should be manufactured. The *Daily Herald* of London enterprisingly inquired of Albert Schweitzer, in Lambaréné, what he thought of Haddow's proposal. Schweitzer, out of character, responded with a short letter or essay. This was published prominently as "The H-Bomb" in that newspaper on April 11, 1954.
9. Albert Schweitzer and Adlai E. Stevenson corresponded at least from 1955 through 1964. They had several mutual friends, including Clara Urquhart. Schweitzer, in perhaps his first letter to the American statesman, in the spring of 1955,

expressed regret that Stevenson could not make a detour on a trip through Africa to visit Lambaréné. He would have been "charmed" by a visit. In June 1957, Stevenson managed to visit Schweitzer at Lambaréné and issued a press statement thereafter. A detailed description of the visit, and conversations, written by Clara Urquhart, exists in the archives. The November 1957 letter by Schweitzer is self-explanatory, coming some months after Stevenson's visit and reflecting some of the topics of their conversation. Permission to quote this correspondence was granted by the Adlai E. Stevenson Papers at the Princeton University Library.

10. Reproduced with permission of the Adlai E. Stevenson Papers in the Princeton University Library. The entire correspondence, on both sides, merits publication.One example is that from Stevenson dated February 8, 1960, reprinted with permission from the Adlai E. Stevenson Papers in the Princeton University Library:

"Your letter came during the Christmas holidays and I found it both comforting and disturbing—comforting because it was reassuring proof that your mind and heart are as vigorous as ever. But I was disturbed because you find so little that is bright and encouraging in your vision of the world. While I have been immeasurably provoked by our failure to reach a comprehensive agreement in nuclear testing at Geneva and get started with inspection, I do find comfort in the fact that we are still negotiating and, indeed, I understand on the threshold of agreement. Is that not an important first step and a breach in the long and dreadful arms limitation deadlock?

"As to those journeys of Chiefs of State and the illusory impression of progress toward peace, I quite agree with your estimate. Moreover, one must view the effect on this institution of the Presidency of this experiment with personal diplomacy with anxiety. Surely, the President can't play all the instruments in the band and do justice to his constitutional task of leadership. But for all I know, conditions have been precarious enough to warrant what President Eisenhower has done and what Khrushchev is now doing—again.

"I think your estimate of the situation between the Soviets and the West is about right, and I look for little progress toward political settlements as long as the positions remain rigid. Nor can I dismiss the Soviet misgivings about German rearmament and missile installations.

"Here in America we still have much to learn. While everyone declares solemnly that peace is his heart's desire and our most important national issue, they are also quick to denounce any accommodation with the Russians as appeasement or softness. I am afraid that most Americans think of peace as peace on our terms and unconditional surrender by the Soviets. Nor do our politicians or press do much to erase this naiveté.

"But, even worse, I am afraid we Americans have a great deal of mythology and self-deceit to penetrate before the realities of the world are clear and reason restored. I think it has been this tendency to constantly reassure our people that all is well and that the present uneasy and precarious situation is peace.

"I wish very much that I could take advantage of your invitation to come to Lambaréné. There is so much to talk about and so little time.

"I pray that you continue well and will find other opportunities to let me have your views. But please don't despair. We are struggling with darkness here and I wish I felt that the Russian leaders were doing as much there.

Sincerely yours,
Adlai E. Stevenson"

11. Reproduced with permission of the Adlai E. Stevenson Papers in the Princeton University Library.

12. Reproduced with permission of the Adlai E. Stevenson Papers in the Princeton University Library.

13. Reproduced with permission of the Adlai E. Stevenson Papers in the Princeton University Library. Stevenson was appointed by President Kennedy in 1961 as Ambassador from the United States to the United Nations. He died in July 1965, two months before Schweitzer. The last extant letter Schweitzer wrote to Stevenson, dated January 2, 1963, was completely devoted to the Katanga issue.

14. Published in *Cahiers del las Reconciliation* (May, 1965) #5; translated by Allen Hackett. Jean Lasserre, a well-known French pacifist and pastor in the Reformed Church, served as Executive Secretary for the M.I.R.

*Legacy*

# 8

# An Abridged Anthology of Schweitzer Quotes

*This chapter contains an anthology of comments by Albert Schweitzer on peace, disarmament, personalities, nuclear tests, and related issues, penned between 1951 and 1965. For lack of space, many more excellent quotations had to be excluded. Each quotation gives the source and the date. The following source abbreviations are used:*

A1 — Appeal, April 28, 1958.
A2 — Appeal, April 29, 1958.
A3 — Appeal, April 30, 1958.
C — Declaration of Conscience, April 23, 1957.
D — *The Daily Herald,* London, April 11, 1954.
G — German Book Trade Association, September 16, 1951.
LC — Letters to Norman Cousins, 1957–1962.
LR — Letters to Bertrand Russell, 1955–1965.
N — Nobel Peace Prize Address, November 4, 1954.

---

ADENAUER, KONRAD

He does not want to talk to anyone. He can hear only people who speak according to his opinion. . . . Public opinion creates great worries in him, more than he is willing to admit. And in me he sees the big enemy, who, because I enjoy great respect in Germany, contributes to this public opinion. Before that, we had a very good relationship with each other. But now I would not dare to visit him because it would cause him pain. (LC 12/4/58)

---

## ATOMIC WAR

In an atomic war there would be neither conqueror nor vanquished. During such a bombardment both sides would suffer the same fate. A continuous destruction would take place and no armistice or peace proposals could bring it to an end. (A2 4/29/58)

When people deal with atomic weapons, no one can say to the other, "Now the arms must decide," but only, "now we want to commit suicide together, destroying each other mutually." (A2 4/29/58)

Those who conduct an atomic war for . . . freedom will die, or end their lives miserably. Instead of freedom they will find destruction. Radioactive clouds resulting from a war between East and West would imperil humanity everywhere. (A2 4/29/58)

An atomic war is . . . the most senseless and lunatic act that could ever take place. At all cost it must be prevented. (A2 4/29/58)

The risk of an atomic war is being increased by the fact that no warning would be given in starting such a war, which could originate in some mere incident. (A2 4/29/58)

At this stage we have the choice of two risks: the one lies in continuing the mad atomic race, with its danger of an unavoidable atomic war in the near future; the other in the renunciation of nuclear weapons, and in the hope that America and the Soviet Union, and the peoples associated with them, will manage to live in peace. The first holds no hope of a prosperous future; the second does. We must risk the second. (A3 4/30/58)

This unexpected and senseless sending of troops to the Middle East has shown the people of Europe that the danger of an atomic war, which can start at any time, really exists. (LC 8/15/58)

An all-out atomic war becomes immediately a world war. And it is necessary to point out to those who declare that they will use atomic weapons their responsibility vis-à-vis the world. (LC 11/11/62)

---

## BERLIN QUESTION

The Berlin question gives the politicians who are the virtuosi of madness an opportunity to withdraw from the nuclear issue. They also never stop to ask themselves whether it is morally right to risk an atomic war over the Berlin question. I wonder how many people are really prepared to die because of Berlin. (LC 3/3/59)

The U.S. should have concerned itself with East Germany's independence and the peace treaty between the Soviets and East Germany, instead of letting the unsolved problem of Berlin continue, which is troubling the whole world. (LC undated 1961)

The Berlin crisis is slowly cooling off. It developed because Kennedy, instead of simply negotiating with the Soviets directly, started a mobilization and a tremendous strengthening of the army. (LC undated 1961)

We in Europe are surprised that in the U.S.A. there is talk of going to war because of Berlin and of the question of fighting and, eventually, dying for Berlin. I do not understand why the diplomats speak of this eventuality. One must be out of one's mind to speak in that fashion. (LC 10/10/61)

In public I never discuss the problem of Berlin, because it is stupid. It does not merit the importance it is being given. (LC 10/10/61)

To think of an atomic war over Berlin is idiocy. . . . And if there is an atomic war because of Berlin, the first thing that will happen is that the two Berlins will cease to exist— thanks to the use of atomic weapons. The Berliners know it and are afraid of a war because of it. . . . Berliners would rather stay alive. (LC 10/31/62)

Nuclear war over Berlin means that within the space of one hour Germany will cease to exist. (LC 11/11/62)

---

## CESSATION OF TESTS

Large-scale experiments might provoke a catastrophe that would endanger the very existence of humanity. Only now does the full horror of our position become clear to us. We can no longer evade the problem of the future of our race. (N 11/4/54)

An end of further experiments with atom bombs would be like the early sunrays of hope which suffering humanity is longing for. (C 4/23/57)

The nations responsible for nuclear tests must renounce them immediately, without making this dependent on a disarmament agreement. (A1 4/28/58)

The two vital issues so essential to the very existence of mankind (are) the cessation of tests and the disposal (use) of nuclear weapons. (A3 4/30/58)

---

## CHINA, PEOPLE'S REPUBLIC OF

Through America's refusal to recognize the real government of China, the (international) situation does not get easier. (LC 8/15/58)

---

## "CLEAN" BOMB

The reassurance propaganda expects much from the glad tidings that science has succeeded in making the prototype of a hydrogen bomb producing far less of dangerous radioactive materials than the usual ones. The new bomb is called "the clean hydrogen bomb." The old type must from now on be content to be called the dirty bomb. (A1 4/28/58)

The clean hydrogen bomb is intended for window-dressing only, not for use. The bomb is to encourage people to believe that future nuclear tests will be followed by less and less radiation, and that there is no argument against the continuation of the tests. (A1 4/28/58)

The new, highly praised hydrogen bomb is—let it be said in passing—only relatively clean.... This bomb, when detonated, also produces radioactivity, as do the neutrons released in great numbers at the explosion. (A1 4/28/58)

COUSINS, NORMAN

At your first visit here ... you tried to convince me that I should speak in regard to atomic weapons. Before, others had talked to me, asked me to do so, without my being able to make a decision. Then you came and asked me the same and it impressed me. So it was you who made me do it, to take up the word for the cause. (LC 8/24/58)

DISARMAMENT

An agreement of this kind (to ban tests) presupposes reliability and trust. There must be guarantees preventing the agreement from being signed by anyone intending to win important tactical advantages. (C 4/23/57)

The fact is that the testing and use of nuclear weapons carry in themselves the absolute reasons for their being renounced. Prior agreement in any other condition cannot be considered.... The three nuclear powers owe it to themselves and to mankind to reach agreement on these essentials without dealing with prior conditions. The negotiations about disarmament are therefore not the forerunner of such agreement, but the outcome of it. They start from the point where agreement on the nuclear issues has been reached, and their goal is to reach the point where the three nuclear powers and the peoples who are connected with them must agree on guarantees that will seek to avert the danger of a threat of a non-atomic nature taking the place of the previous danger. (A3 4/30/58)

Should agreement be reached on the outlawing of nuclear weapons, this alone . . . will have led to a great improvement in the political situation, because as a result of such an agreement time and distance would again become realities in their own rights. Nuclear arms give a distant war the effect of a near war. (A3 4/30/58)

Disarmament discussions between the three nuclear powers must concern themselves with guarantees that actual, total, and irrevocable disposal of nuclear weapons will be secured. The problem of effective control will also have to be anticipated. Reciprocal agreement will have to be reached on permitting international commissions to investigate on national soil. (A3 4/30/58)

If negotiations on disarmament are held, not as a preliminary to the renunciation of nuclear arms but as a result of it, they would have a much larger meaning. . . . Disarmament and all questions leading to a stable situation . . . could be discussed much better after agreement had been reached on the renunciation of atomic weapons. (A3 4/30/58)

If in our time we renounce nuclear arms we shall have taken the first step on the way to the distant goal of the end to all wars. If we do not do this we remain on the road that leads in the near future to atomic war and misery. (A3 4/30/58)

I give my opinion only on the problem of disarmament and peace! This is the real problem. And it is there that the people ought to raise their voices. (LC 10/10/61)

An urgent necessity for the world is that the atomic powers agree as soon as possible on disarmament under effective international control. The possibility of such disarmament negotiations should not be made questionable by unnecessary appeals for international verification of the discontinuance of testing. Only when the states agree not to carry out tests any more can promising negotiations about disarmament and peace take place. (Letter to John F. Kennedy 4/20/62)

Time works for those of us who wish to abolish nuclear weapons. The world will see that nuclear weapons are a burden of which we must relieve ourselves. (LC 10/22/62)

There have been negotiations about the abolition of atomic weapons. We assume that while these negotiations are taking place, no civilized country would decide to use atomic weapons. Now the U.S.A takes this step! . . .Therefore, these negotiations about atomic weapons are losing their meaning. (LR 10/24/62)

---

## DULLES, JOHN FOSTER

There is now an uneasiness in Europe that the policy of Dulles is not satisfactory. That American newspapers criticize him very much also makes an impression in Europe. (LC 8/15/58)

And then (Lewis L.) Strauss and (Edward) Teller made such blunders that Dulles could not hold with them anymore. (LC 8/24/58)

I believe that the silly word by Dulles, that Berlin is the Quemoy of Europe, is responsible for Khrushchev's action. (LC 11/24/58)

People are beginning to be more reasonable than they were before in their judgment of communism. The anti-communism of the Dulles period is beginning to falter. (LR 10/18/62)

---

## ECONOMIC CONSEQUENCES

The unlimited production of nuclear weapons can be ruinous to the economy. One can no longer go into the construction of nuclear arms in order to maintain one's supremacy. The economy will no longer permit it. Nuclear weapons are beginning to be a grave problem, one that will continue, year after year, to undermine economies. (LC 11/22/62)

---

## EINSTEIN, ALBERT

I thought of Einstein—what it would have meant to him if he could have lived to see the day which he longed for so much (moratorium on nuclear tests). (LC 8/24/58)

---

## GENETIC DAMAGE

The meaning of the obscure statement that the "effects on heredity if the increase in radioactivity of the air are kept within tolerable limits" is that the number of children who will be born deformed, as a result of the harm done to the sexual cells, supposedly will not be large enough to justify the stopping of the tests. (Al 4/28/58)

We are constantly being told about "a permissible amount of radiation." Who permitted it? Who has any right to permit it? (Al 4/28/58)

The most sinister aspect of both internal and external radiation is that years may pass before the evil consequences appear. Indeed, they make themselves felt, not in the first or second generation, but in the following ones. Generation after generation, for centuries to come, will witness the birth of an ever-increasing number of children with mental and physical defects. (Al 4/28/58)

The scientists declared that the radioactivity gradually created by nuclear tests represents a greater danger for all parts of the world, particularly serious because its consequence will be an increasing number of deformed children in the future. (Al 4/28/58)

One incomprehensible aspect of the propaganda for the continuation of nuclear tests is its complete disregard of their harmful effects on future generations which, according to biologists and physicians, will be the result of the radiation to which we are being exposed. (A1 4/28/58)

We must not be responsible for the future birth of thousands of children with the most serious mental and physical defects, simply because we did not pay enough attention to that danger. Only those who have never been present at the birth of a deformed baby, never witnessed the whimpering shock of its mother, dare to maintain that the risk in going on with nuclear tests is one which must be taken under existing circumstances. (A1 4/28/58)

---

## HISTORY

That the present situation is impossible, alike for victors and for vanquished, is due to our neglect of historical reality. We have not taken proper notice of history, and, in consequence, we no longer know what is just—or what is useful. (N 11/4/54)

---

## HUMAN SPIRIT

The spirit of humanity is a creative spirit and therefore we trust in it not only because it remains our hope in these times, but because it is able to fulfill its historic task. (G 9/16/51)

The spirit of humanity can develop in ourselves because we all possess the material out of which it strives to develop, that is, the consciousness of our highest human ability and vocation in ourselves. (G 9/16/51)

Humanity cannot develop in the world if it fails to develop in every individual and if we don't dare to give it sufficient space in ourselves and in our lives. The spirit has to become a fact everywhere where there is no peace. Absence of peace not only exists between peoples but also within people themselves, and the spirit will prove its existence when it dares to attack the basis of this absence of peace between peoples. (G 9/16/51)

The only originality which I claim for myself is . . . that the human spirit in our time is capable of creating a new attitude of mind: an attitude based on ethics. (N 11/4/54)

Today we must once again abandon ourselves—if we do not wish to go to our destruction—to that pristine strength of the human spirit. . . . The human spirit is not dead: it lives on in secret. (N 11/4/54)

We cannot continue in this paralyzing mistrust. If we want to work our way out of the desperate situation in which we find ourselves another spirit must enter into the people. It can only come if the awareness of its necessity suffices to give us strength to believe in its coming. We must presuppose the awareness of this need in all peoples who have suffered along with us. We must approach them in the spirit that we are human beings, all of us, and that we feel ourselves fitted to feel with each other; to think and to will together in the same way. (A3 4/30/58)

The awareness that we are all human beings together has become lost in war and through politics. . . . Now we must re-discover the fact that we—all together—are human beings, and that we must strive to concede to each other what moral capacity we have. Only in this way can we begin to believe that in other peoples as well as in ourselves there will arise the need for a new spirit, which can be the beginning of a feeling of mutual trustworthiness towards each other. The spirit is a mighty force for transforming things. (A3 4/30/58)

In President Eisenhower's speech following the launching of the Sputnik on 7th November 1957, he said, "What the world needs more than a gigantic leap into space is a gigantic leap into peace." This gigantic leap consists in finding the courage to hope that the spirit of good sense will arise in individuals and in peoples, a spirit sufficiently strong to overcome the insanity and inhumanity. (A3 4/30/58)

## ILLEGALITY OF NUCLEAR OF WEAPONS

Nuclear weapons are against international law and they have to be abolished for that reason irrespective of whether or not the three atomic powers have come to a satisfactory disarmament agreement, because in peace and in war they harm the uninvolved people and even humanity. (LC 4/14/58)

Our purpose in expressing the argument that atomic weapons contradict international law is to arm the hands of the opponents of atomic weapons, or their mouths, in order that they may shout it all over the world. It is evident that atomic weapons are contrary to international law. People will believe it because of its evidence and because it is based on human and moral reflections. (LC 5/17/58)

All weapons which produce radioactivity, even those which are being praised as clean, have to be looked on as opposed to the *Völkerrecht* (international law) and must be abandoned. (LC 8/15/58)

The argument that atomic weapons are against the law of the people (*Völkerrecht*) finds more and more recognition, and that the meaning of this is well understood. (LC 8/15/58)

We must carry on with our new argument that they (nuclear weapons) are against human rights. . . . We must stress the legal moral argument. The human rights declaration was based not only on legal but also on moral grounds, and it is for moral reasons that we must make our stand against extinction. The fact that law is based on morality is the decisive thing in this case and must be brought to the fore. (LC 3/3/59)

---

## INTERNATIONAL LAW

It is strange that so far nobody has stressed that the question of whether nuclear tests should be stopped or continued is not one which concerns the nuclear powers exclusively, a question for them to decide at pleasure. (A1 4/28/58)

Who is giving these countries (the nuclear powers) the right to experiment, in time of peace, with weapons involving the most serious risks for the whole world? (A1 4/28/58)

What has international law—enthroned by the UN and so highly praised in our time—to say on this matter (cessation of tests)? Does it no longer look out on the world from its temple? Then take it out (of its temple) that it may face the facts and do its duty accordingly. (A1 4/28/58)

More guilty however is international law, which has kept silent and indifferent on this question (cessation of tests), year after year. (A1 4/28/58)

The question of continuing or ceasing nuclear tests is an urgent matter for international law. (A1 4/28/58)

The main thing now is to distribute as widely as possible the idea that the atomic weapons are against international law, because the cessation of atomic tests can only be achieved with this argument. (LC 9/24/58)

The jurists, in common secret accord, have not occupied themselves with this question (that atomic weapons are against international law) in order not to be obligated to give evidence as to the illegality regarding international law, which they say is the duty of governments. (Letter to Casals, 11/22/58)

---

## INTERNATIONAL PEACE MOVEMENT

I do not think that a conference of scientists is what is needed. . . . There are too many conferences in the world today and too many decisions taken by them. (D 4/14/54)

I could . . . help in the creation of the general movement if I judge that my intervention would serve a purpose . . . Sustain the movement in America and it will propagate itself in Europe, and in the world. And count on me for everything that I will be able to do to propagate the movement. (LC 11/11/57)

Our propaganda is passed on from man to man, its strength is that it represents what is true and sensible. Our propaganda has dignity. It works with simple means; it is noble.

This we may not abandon and we must not ever adjust to a propaganda which uses any available means. We are prophets of the truth who can save the world. (LR 10/18/62)

---

KENNEDY, JOHN F.

Kennedy will be pleased if he is not mentioned (by Schweitzer and Russell). He will be penitent when he is spared the humiliation of a public judgment. (LR 11/11/62)

---

KHRUSHCHEV, NIKITA

Khrushchev has a difficult time with China and . . . America and England should take this to heart and not make more difficulties. (LC 8/15/58)

The people have had to admit that Khrushchev kept calm and that he did not answer the unnecessary sending of troops (to the Middle East by the U.S.A. and the U.K.) with sending of troops on his part. (LC 8/15/58)

Naturally, this is a very unfriendly action (in Berlin) on the part of Khrushchev, not a bit suited to helping the situation in which we live. (LC 11/24/58)

I consider it also a valuable achievement that all have to acknowledge that Khrushchev wants peace. (LR 10/18/62)

And what would have become of you, and of us with you, if Khrushchev had not put aside all question of prestige and simply offered to surrender (in the Cuban crisis). (LC 11/11/62)

I know that Khrushchev is not concerned with prestige, as is Kennedy and others, and could (also) make concessions if it should be necessary to keep the peace. And this is what actually happened. Kennedy has to be grateful to him for this, for the rest of his life, since Khrushchev saved him from the terrible situation he had gotten into because of his policy of strength. Nations cannot help (otherwise) but listen attentively in astonishment as to how he saved the peace in such a simple way. (LR 11/11/62)

---

### LAWYERS

My hope is that among the lawyers in the world there will be some to open their mouths... We don't need the lawyers' blessings. History shows how it is their role to pour water into the neat wine of the law of humanity and to construct compromises. (LC 5/17/58)

The lawyers would have been the ones to use and raise the argument (in the World Court) that atomic weapons contradict the law of humanity; but they were silent and have failed. Therefore we will leave them out of the game. They would be but unreliable allies. Keep away from lawyers. Keep away from courts. (LC 5/17/58)

I am fighting against the atomic danger; but it is not up to me to judge the lawyers and the Pope. (LC 5/17/58)

Until now lawyers have shied away from questions that were unsympathetic to the governments; they have just not lived up to occupying themselves with this. But now, when everywhere this question has been discussed, they cannot do otherwise but to occupy themselves with it. (LC 8/15/58)

---

### LODGE, HENRY CABOT

An American representative (to the UN) who professes such a false opinion (about radioactive fallout) in the name of America. (LC 10/14/57)

---

## McNamara, Robert

We must, in our struggle against nuclear weapons, criticize the fact that McNamara did something very grave in announcing that he would use all forces—that is to say nuclear arms as well—in a war over the problem of Cuba or of Berlin. If we are really fighting against nuclear arms, we cannot abstain from criticizing McNamara, severely and publicly. Otherwise, we fail in our duty. We cannot make concessions. (LC 10/31/62)

---

## Meddling

I don't want to give the impression that I am meddling in U.S.A. affairs. (LC 10/14/57)

You will remember how I refused to slip into the anti-atom movement with my name, in the U.S.A. The same principle holds everywhere. . . . The fight in one's own country has to be fought by each one in one's own country. (LC 12/4/58)

People do not tolerate it lightly when their head of state is criticized. (LR 11/11/62)

---

## Moratorium

The handicap of not being able to try out new (weapons) would be the same for all (nuclear powers). (Al 4/28/58)

The immediate renunciation of further tests will create a favorable atmosphere for talks on banning the use of nuclear weapons. When this urgently necessary step has been taken, such negotiations can take place in peace. (Al 4/28/58)

That the Soviets renounced the tests was put down as propaganda and made hardly any impression. (LC 8/24/58)

I believe that no atomic power would now dare to start testing again. (LC 3/3/59)

The resumption of nuclear testing was the temptation to which East and West had to succumb. The Soviets were the first to succumb. It was they who shocked the world and who shall bear the consequences of world public opinion. The U.S.A., in resuming tests, can say that the Soviets made it a necessity. (LC 10/30/61)

It is deplorable, it is terrible, it is agonizing. We are sinking ever more deeply into inhumanity by the resumption of tests. For thousands of men are condemned to suffer and to die from nuclear radiation, and generations of newborn children will continue in increasing numbers to be deformed, incapable of living. (LC 10/30/61)

---

## MOVEMENT OF POPULATIONS

We await the first sign of that manifestation of the spirit in which we must place our trust. This sign can only take one form; the beginnings of an attempt by every nation to repair, as far as possible, the wrongs which each inflicted upon the other during the last war. Hundreds of thousands of prisoners and deportees are still wanting to go back to their homes. (N 11/4/54)

The most flagrant violation of the rights of history—and, above all, the rights of man—occurs when a people is deprived of the right to the land on which it lives and has to move elsewhere. (N 11/4/54)

Of all the very difficult problems the future holds, the most difficult will be the rights of access of over-populated countries to neighboring lands. (A3 4/30/58)

---

## NATIONALISM

The worst kind of nationalism has manifested itself during the two wars and is at this moment the greatest obstacle to international understanding. This nationalism can only be overthrown by the rebirth, in all mankind, of a humanitarian ideal; attachment to one's fatherland would then become natural, healthful, and ideal in character. (N 11/4/54)

(After) the middle of the nineteenth century . . . national self-consciousness became more and more intense; and the consequences were grave. Nations could no longer be guided by reason and historical truth. (N 11/4/54)

---

## NORTH ATLANTIC TREATY ORGANIZATION (NATO)

We have to keep the NATO generals from forcing launching pads and nuclear weapons on the governments, which would amount to a military isolation of the Soviet Union and which could lead to war. We cannot and will not tolerate this NATO domination, which does not at all consider the abolition of nuclear weapons but only the continuation of armament . . . NATO has wanted to force nuclear weapons on us. . . . The American government may know that public opinion does not agree with its policy on nuclear weapons for NATO and that it puts pressure on the European governments from which they cannot escape. (LC 4/14/58)

The unnatural situation created by the two world wars that led to a (U.S.) dominating military presence in Europe cannot continue indefinitely. It must gradually cease to exist, both for the sake of Europe and for the sake of America. (A3 4/30/58)

That neither the U.S.A. nor England thought it necessary to let the other countries belonging to NATO to know about their decided adventure (in the Middle East in 1958) has harmed the reputation of NATO very much. (LC 8/15/58)

NATO has arrived at a point where only an atomic war is being considered. But atomic weapons are not defenses. . . . They are aggressive. (LC 11/24/58)

---

## PARLIAMENTS

The parliaments cannot be relied on in this matter (opposing nuclear weapons). They are completely without an opinion and therefore also completely irresponsible in the matter of this great danger in which the nations find themselves. Yet 15 years ago one could not have imagined such behavior of parliaments. Today it is accepted as something that is part of our time. (LR 6/27/62)

---

## PAULING, LINUS

Much good work was done by the courageous and knowledgeable Pauling, who kept questioning Teller and did not rest until it was proved that . . . a seismograph as far as Alaska had registered the disturbance—contrary to what was said at the time. (LC 8/24/58)

It meant a lot that Pauling was successful in getting a manifesto from 9,326 scientists (who until August 1958 were condemned to silence). (LC 8/24/58)

---

## PEACE TREATY

The second world war has not been followed by any treaty of peace. The agreements which brought it to an end had the character merely of a truce . . . . and cannot be regarded as in any way permanent. (N 11/4/54)

---

## POLITICAL PROPAGANDA

What a sad time we're living in! Falsehood rises up in the name of facts against truth, which the latter cannot manifest itself as it should because the lie is joined with well-organized publicity. (LC 10/14/57)

The declaration signed by 9,235 scientists of all nations. . . gave the reassurance propaganda (of governments) its death-blow. (A1 4/28/58)

Later the slogan appeared in America and in Europe simultaneously that one must be able to live with the atomic bomb and that one can live with the atomic bomb. (LC 8/24/58)

It is our culture which tolerates these circumstances, and does not acquire any knowledge because those who reign feel uncomfortable about it—they don't like to be open about it, they don't allow the public to know the truth about the dangers of the atomic age. These are strange circumstances under which we live. (LC 9/24/58)

Again propaganda dared to advocate holding on to atomic weapons, trying to calm public opinion. (LC 11/24/58)

You know as well as I do that the big obstacle to forming this public opinion in the West is that governments want to prevent the development of this opinion and use as a weapon calling those who support this opinion as being suspect of being communist. This defamation is the most horrible weapon all those who are dependent have to fear. (LR 6/27/62)

Everyone who declares himself against atomic weapons in Europe and the U.S.A. is considered a bad person. (LR 9/2/62)

---

POPE PIUS XII

Also the Pope (Pius XII) we will leave alone. He is a great sir, and he owes consideration to the church. He may be a good man, but he is no fighter. Or did you ever read anywhere that he condemned the atomic and H bombs in the name of Christian religion? Protestantism does it, but there is no Catholic declaration so far. (LC 5/17/58)

---

PRESS

The press does not disturb us with editorials drawing our attention to and making us share in what lies behind such news (radioactive contamination in Japan)—the misery of the Japanese people. Thus we and the press are made guilty of lack of compassion. (A1 4/28/58)

The American and European press is constantly receiving abundant propaganda material supplied by government atomic commissions and scientists who feel called upon to support this view (that nuclear tests are necessary). (A1 4/28/58)

Radio and the press are the small firewood to kindle a fire, booklets which are passed from one hand to the next are the big logs to keep the fire burning and to bring it to its full effect. (LC 5/17/58)

It mattered greatly that your magazine (*The Saturday Review*) again and again backed the truth. (LC 8/24/58)

Public opinion cannot do anything because the press which should deal with these things does not dare to pick up the word. (LC 9/24/58)

That the press remains indifferent also in this issue (atomic weapons are against human rights) is quite natural, but we, the fighters, must keep shouting about it. (LC 3/3/59)

Also the newspapers are not conscious of their responsibility. They have no opinion, but behave purely as reporters. (LR 6/27/62)

---

PRIORITIES

Despite all the political happenings which have pressed themselves into the foreground, the nuclear question demands prior attention. (LC 11/24/58)

The political happenings of recent times have pushed the atomic question completely into the background, which is a fact of great value to those who are pro-atom. It is indeed very sad . . . that the atomic question steps back behind political questions . . . The atomic question became a dish of soup which one removes from the table to warm up the kitchen. (LC 11/24/58)

_____

## PUBLIC OPINION

Public opinion . . . stands in no need of plebiscites or of forming of committees to express itself. It works through just being there. (C 4/23/57)

Why do they (the three nuclear weapons states) not come to an agreement (to stop nuclear tests)? The real reason is that in their own countries there is no public opinion asking for it. Nor is there any such public opinion in other countries, with the exception of Japan. (C 4/23/57)

This propaganda (for the continuation of nuclear tests) will continue to set the tone in certain newspapers. But beside it the truth about the danger of nuclear tests marches imperturbably along, influencing an ever-increasing section of public opinion. In the long run, even the most efficiently organized propaganda can do nothing against the truth. (A1 4/28/58)

People are becoming increasingly aware of dangers resulting from nuclear tests. (A1 4/28/58)

The time is past when a European country could plan secretly to establish itself as a great power by manufacturing atomic weapons exclusively for its own use. Since public opinion would never agree to such an undertaking, it becomes senseless even to prepare secretly for the realization of such a plan. Past too is the time when NATO generals and European governments can decide on the establishment of launching-sites and the stockpiling of atomic weapons. The dangers of atomic war, and its consequences, are now such that these decisions have ceased to be purely matters of politics and can be valid only with the sanction of public opinion. (A2 4/29/58)

Our task is to raise our voices permanently in order to awake those who are still asleep and to build up a public opinnion which is capable of bearing pressure upon the governments. (LC 5/17/58)

The American "calming" propaganda, with Teller and Strauss and the Atomic Energy Commission, had such a terrific success in America and in Europe, that public opinion was chloroformed and the press was apathetic. (LC 8/24/58)

We were able at least to create a public opinion which forced the politicians to capitulate. (LC 9/24/58)

That must now be our only goal—to create this enlightened and cohesive public opinion. It is in this arena that the battle must be joined. (LC 3/3/59)

All negotiations regarding the abolition of atomic weapons remain without success because no international public opinion exists which demands this abolition . . . In all propaganda against atomic weapons . . . I speak of the necessity of a strong public opinion in the world. (LR 6/27/62)

---

RADIOACTIVE FALLOUT

Testing of atomic weapons is something quite different from testing of non-atomic ones. (C 4/23/57)

We are forced to regard every increase in the existing danger through further creation of radioactive elements by atom bomb explosions as a catastrophe for the human race, a catastrophe that must be prevented. (C 4/23/57)

Individuals and peoples have not been aroused to give to this danger the attention which it unfortunately deserves. (C 4/23/57)

Radiation resulting from the explosions which have already taken place represents a danger to the human race—a danger not to be underrated—and that further explosions of atomic bombs will increase this danger to an alarming extent. (C 4/23/57)

Every new nuclear test makes a bad situation worse. (A1 4/28/58)

Even without new tests the danger will increase during the coming years: a large part of the radioactive elements flung up in the atmosphere and stratosphere at the nuclear experiments is still there. It will come down only after several years, probably about 15. (A1 4/28/58)

---

## REVERENCE FOR LIFE

The spirit of humanity . . . refers not only to its fellow man but encompasses everything in its domain. It needs no knowledge of life and the world, other than knowing that everything which exists in life, and of recognizing that we must regard with the greatest reverence all life as being of the most precious and irreplaceable value. (G 9/16/51)

Compassion, in which all ethics must take root, can only attain its full breadth and depth if it embraces all living creatures and does not limit itself to mankind. Ancient ethics had not this depth, this strength of conviction, but beside it there now stands a new ethic—that of respect for life, whose validity is more and more widely acknowledged. (N 11/4/54)

---

## SCIENTISTS

Everywhere in the world people fear for peace and. . .the fate of mankind is in the balance. But where does this fear—this confusion in which we find ourselves—stem from? It stems from the power gained by the progress in man's knowledge and his increased technical capabilities. (G 9/16/51)

It must be the scientists, who comprehend thoroughly all the issues and the dangers involved (of radioactivity from nuclear tests) who speak to the world, as many as possible of them all telling humanity the truth in speeches and articles. If they all raised their voices, each one feeling himself impelled to tell the terrible truth, they would be listened to, for then humanity would understand that the issues were grave. . . . If (they) can put before mankind the thoughts by which they themselves are obsessed, then there will be some hope of stopping these horrible explosions and of bringing pressure to bear on the men who govern. (D 4/14/54)

The scientists must speak up. Only they have the authority to state that we can no longer take on ourselves the responsibility for these experiments, only they can say it. (D 4/14/54)

Man has become superman. . . . But this superman suffers from a fatal imperfection of mind. He has not raised himself to that superhuman level of reason which should correspond to the possession of superhuman strength. Yet it is this that he needs, if he is to put his gigantic strength to ends which are reasonable and useful, rather than destructive and murderous. For this reason the advance of science has become fatal to him, rather than advantageous. (N 11/4/54)

The strength (of the human mind) later diminished— above all because of the researchers of science failed to establish any ethical foundation beneath our vastly increased knowledge of the world. Man no longer knew quite in which direction he should progress. His ideals grew less lofty. (N 11/9/54)

It is a sad thing that the scientists of the West did not have the courage to say that the tests must be stopped on account of the scientific reports. They were forced by their governments to take that attitude, to leave the decision to the politicians. It does not give honor to the West that its scientists were resigned to leaving the verdict to the politicians and not to expressing their views based on scientific findings. (LC 9/24/58)

## TELLER, EDWARD

Edward Teller, the father of the dirty hydrogen bomb, sang a hymn of praise to the idyllic nuclear war to be waged with completely clean hydrogen bombs. He insists on a continuation of the tests, to perfect this ideal bomb. (A1 4/28/58)

It is not for the physicist, choosing to take into account only the radiation from the air, to say the decisive word on the dangers of nuclear tests. (A1 4/28/58)

Teller was the bad spirit to which President Eisenhower and Dulles bowed. He was the one who influenced them to shatter the London (disarmament) conference, which had been going along all right. . . . He had made them think that by continuing the tests one would arrive at the production of a "clean" hydrogen bomb. . . . That it was necessary for Dulles to separate himself from Teller refuted the "calming" propaganda, which had tried to create the idea of an idyllic atomic war as well as the fiction of "purity of air" with the new tests. (LC 8/24/58)

----

## TRUST

We will only find a way out (of further war) when we can trust one another, when each nation is convinced that the other will not use its power for destructive purposes. But how shall we gain one another's trust? The only possible way is by having the courage to devote ourselves again to a belief in humanity. (G 9/16/51)

----

## U.S.S.R. POLICY

Perhaps the Soviet Union is not quite so malicious as to think only of throwing itself on Europe at the first opportunity in order to devour it, and perhaps not quite so unintelligent as to fail to consider whether there would be any advantage in upsetting her stomach with this indigestible meal. (A3 4/30/58)

This (political restraint in the Middle East) led many people to think about the question, whether the free world is really so much endangered by the Soviets as it is being preached all over the West. (LC 8/15/58)

---

## UNITED NATIONS

The League of Nations and the United Nations . . . have not brought about a state of general peace. Their efforts were bound to fail, because the world in which they operated was in no wise bent upon the achievement of such a peace; and they themselves, being merely juridical institutions, had no power to create a more apposite state of mind. (N 11/4/54)

Only to the extent in which the peoples of the world foster within themselves the ideal of peace will those institutions whose object is the preservation of that peace be able to function as we expect, and hope, that they will. (N 11/4/54)

I cannot understand that the UN cannot make up its mind to bring the matter to a discussion (the question of new atomic tests) . . . We cannot dictate anything to the UN. It is an autonomous body and has to find in itself the incentive and feeling of responsibility to try to prevent a threatening disaster. From the distance I cannot judge what prevents them to rise to the occasion. And if the attempt proved fruitless it would at least have been undertaken and it would have revealed where the opposition is. (Letter to Einstein 2/20/55)

It is an organization that functions in complicated ways. (LC 4/22/57)

---

## U.S. PEACE MOVEMENT

That Americans come out against the opinion of American politics is the beginning of the beginning. (LC 11/11/57)

---

## U.S. POLICY

We no longer wish to be associated with the idea that America keeps the free world free by the threat of nuclear war.... But I talk (in my broadcasts) with affection about the U.S.A. and the (economic) help she has given Europe. (LC 4/14/58)

America has deviated from her principle not to put atomic weapons into the hands of other countries, a decision with grave consequences. (A2 4/29/58)

It would be of immense importance if America in this hour of destiny could decide in favor of renouncing atomic weapons, to remove the possibility of an eventual outbreak of an atomic war. The theory of peace through terrifying an opponent by a greater armament can now only heighten the danger of war. (A2 4/29/58)

In the U.S. it has been decided to use nuclear arms for the questions of Cuba and Berlin. This is a new and serious decision. I should never have thought that the government would dare to take this decision, such a serious one. And I am of the opinion that we must not accept this decision without protesting. (LC 10/22/62)

And McNamara and Kennedy should destroy this perspective (an improved atmosphere in disarmament negotiations) for us by their utilization of atomic weapons? Is the U.S.A. really in agreement with their intentions? Does public opinion in America go along with them? ... These two in America must know that we will not yield! (LR 10/24/62)

You know how much I love America. (LC 11/11/62)

---

## URGENCY

That the reign of peace will eventually come to pass ... has been discounted as "utopian," but the situation today is such that it must in one way or another become reality if humanity is not to perish. (N 11/4/54)

We no longer have the great length of time on which he (Immanuel Kant) was counting for the evolution of peace. The wars of our time, unlike anything he envisaged, are wars of total destruction. We must act decisively, if we are to secure peace. We must get decisive results, and get them soon. Only the spirit can do this. (N 11/4/54)

Our descendants . . . are threatened by the greatest and most terrible danger. . . . To fail to consider (the) importance and (the) consequences (of fallout) would be a folly for which humanity would have to pay a terrible price. We are committing a folly in thoughtlessness. It must not happen that we do not pull ourselves together before it is too late. We must muster the insight, the seriousness, and the courage to leave folly and to face reality. (C 4/23/57)

Mankind is imperilled by the tests. Mankind insists that they stop and has every right to do so. (A1 4/28/58)

There is no time to lose. New tests increasing the danger must not be allowed to take place. (A1 4/28/58)

We have to keep on fighting the battle for the abolition of the tests. (LC 8/24/58)

One can speak a lot of foolishness in politics, but we have to remember that we can all be wiped out by a bomb in a few minutes. (LC 10/10/61)

My hope is that, by the gravity of the situation created by the resumption of tests, men throughout the world will under- stand that they must arrive at a solution to the problem of the terrible danger in which humanity is placed. They can no long- er let things go as they have been doing. We must understand that we are risking the terrible catastrophe in which humanity will perish. (LC 10/30/61)

Let us continue our struggle against nuclear arms; let us not be discouraged by the weariness of former companions in the struggle. (LC 10/22/62)

We must fight. We will not let nuclear war come so simply into the world today. Let us struggle. (LC 11/22/62)

---

WAR

There cannot, at the present time, be any question of "humanizing" war. (N 11/4/54)

Modern warfare is fought out with weapons which are incomparably more destructive than those of the past. War is, in fact, a greater evil than ever before. (N 11/4/54)

The statesmen who reshaped the world . . . did not aim to create situations which might, in time, have resulted in an era of general prosperity; their main effort was to exploit the consequences of victory and, if possible, to make them permanent. (N 11/4/54)

We tolerate mass-killing in wartime—about 20 million people died in the second world war—just as we tolerate the destruction by atomic bombing of whole towns and their populations. . . . When we admit to ourselves that they were the direct results of an act of inhumanity, our admission is qualified by the reflection that "war is war" and there is nothing to be done about it. In so resigning ourselves, without any further resistance, we ourselves become guilty of inhumanity. The important thing is that we should one and all acknowledge that we have been guilty of this inhumanity. The horror of that avowal must needs arouse everyone of us from our torpor, and compel us to hope and work with all our strength for the coming of an age in which war will no longer exist. (N 11/4/54)

It was once possible to regard (war) as an evil to which we could resign ourselves, because it was the servant of progress—and was even essential to it. It could be argued in those days that, thanks to war, those nations which were strongest got the better of their weaker neighbors and thus determined the march of history. (N 11/4/54)

Modern warfare is such that one would hesitate a long time before claiming that it contributes to progress. It constitutes an evil—and an evil far greater than in former times. (N11/4/54)

## War Resistance

Now that we know how terrible an evil war is in our time, we should neglect nothing that may prevent its recurrence. (N 11/4/54)

We should reject war for ethical reasons—because, that is to say, it makes us guilty of the crime of inhumanity. (N 11/4/54)

May the nations, in their efforts to keep peace in being, go to the farthest limits of possibility so that the spirit of man shall be given time to develop and grow strong—and time to act. (N11/4/54)

The menacing possibility of an outbreak of atomic war between Soviet Russia and America . . . can only be avoided if the two powers decide to renounce atomic arms. (A2 4/29/58)

You are absolutely right in organizing the protest marches. (LR 9/2/61)

You . . . have no real conception of the effect your demonstrations have in the world! Continue with them! . . . there are many people today who have doubts about the dominating public opinion, but will not openly admit it. (LR 10/18/62)

Your demonstrations, which have the significance of confessions, have been successful in the past and will continue to be so in the future. This is kind of natural propaganda from one human being to another. (LR 11/18/62)

---

## Women

It is the particular duty of women to prevent this sin (birth defects from radioactive fallout) against the future. It is for them to raise their voices against it in such a way that they will be heard. (A1 4/28/58)

---

WORLD COURT

If this court were efficient, it would raise its voice (against nuclear tests) by itself. But it is not allowed to do so. It is allowed only to judge complaints brought before it by governments. (LC 5/17/58)

# 9
# Albert Schweitzer and the Atomic Age
# A Chronology

1875, January 14—Born in Kaysersberg, Alsace, Germany
1913, March—Embarked at Bordeaux for first sojourn in Africa

1945-Schweitzer's seventieth year

1945, July—First US nuclear weapons test
1945, August—US bombed Hiroshima and Nagasaki
1948, October—To Europe for first time since beginning of World War II
1949, June/July—First and only trip to the US
1949, September—First USSR nuclear weapons test
1949, October—To Africa for eighth sojourn
1951, June—To Europe
1951, September—Accepted German Peace Prize at Frankfurt
1951, December—To Africa for ninth sojourn
1952, July—To Europe
1952, October—First UK nuclear weapons test
1952, December—To Africa for tenth sojourn
1953, November—Awarded 1952 Nobel Peace Prize at Oslo in absentia
1954, March—Nuclear weapons tests at Bikini began worldwide concern over radiation fallout

1954, June—To Europe
1954, November—Accepted Nobel Peace Prize at Oslo
1954, December—To Africa for eleventh sojourn

1955—Schweitzer's Eightieth Year—59 atomic
tests by three countries

1955, July—To Europe
1955, October—Met Bertrand Russell in London
1955, December—To Africa for twelfth sojourn
1957, January—Norman Cousins visited Lambaréné
1957, April—Declaration of Conscience broadcast from
Radio Oslo
1957, June—To Europe
1957, December—To Africa for thirteenth sojourn
1958, April—Three addresses broadcast from Radio
Oslo
1959, August—To Europe
1959, December—To Africa for fourteenth and final
sojourn
1960, October—First French nuclear weapons test
1963, August—Partial nuclear test-ban treaty signed
1964, October—First Chinese nuclear weapons test

1965—Ninetieth Year—624 tests
by five countries

1965, September 4—Died at Lambaréné, Gabon

# 10

# A Selected Reading List

*T*his chapter is an abridged list of the major volumes written by or about Albert Schweitzer and, with one exception, translated into English. The initial date is that of the original publication.

A. MAJOR WORKS OF ALBERT SCHWEITZER, Listed Chronologically.

*1898* Eugene Munch, 1857–1895. In *Music in the Life of Albert Schweitzer,* ed. by Charles R. Joy. New York: Harper. Boston: Beacon Press, 1951. 300pp. Freeport, N.Y.:Books for Libraries Press, 1971. 300pp.

*1899* *The Essence of Faith: Philosophy of Religion,* ed. by Kurt F. Leidecker. New York: Philosophical Library and Book Sales, 1966. 124pp.

*1901* *The Mystery of the Kingdom of God: The Secret of Jesus' Messiahship and Passion.* New York: Schocken Books, 1970. 275pp. Buffalo: Prometheus, 1985.

*1906* "The Art of Organ Playing in Germany and France." In *Music in the Life of Albert Schweitzer,* ed. by Charles R. Joy. New York: Harper. Boston: Beacon Press, 1951. 300pp. Freeport, N.Y.: Books for Libraries Press, 1971. 300pp.

*1906* *The Quest of the Historical Jesus. A Critical Study of its Progress from Reimarus to Wrede.* New York: Macmillan, 1968. 413pp.

*1908* *J. S. Bach.* New York: Dover, 1966. 2 vol. 428pp. 498pp.

*1911* *Paul and His Interpreters: A Critical History.* New York: Schocken, 1964. 255pp.

1912 *Johann Sebastian Bach. Complete Organ Works.* (With Edouard Nies-Berger.) New York: G. Schirmer, 1912–67. 8 volumes.

1913 *Psychiatric Study of Jesus, Exposition and Criticism.* Boston: Beacon Press, 1948. 81pp. Magnolia, Mass.: Peter Smith, 1958. 81pp.

1921 *On the Edge of the Primeval Forest. The Experiences and Observations of a Doctor in Equatorial Africa.* Cleveland, Ohio: Collins-World, 1976. 126pp. New York: AMS, 1976.

1923 *The Philosophy of Civilization.* New York: Macmillan, 1960. Two parts. 347pp. University Presses of Florida, 1981.

1924 *Memoirs of Childhood and Youth.* New York: Macmillan, 1963. 124pp.

1925 *More From the Primeval Forest.* Cleveland: Collins-World, 1976. 128pp.

1928-1932 *Goethe: Five Studies,* ed. by Charles R. Joy. Boston: Beacon Press, 1961. 143pp.

1930 *The Mysticism of Paul the Apostle.* New York: Seabury, 1968. 411pp.

1931 *Out of My Life and Thought.* New York: Holt, Rinehart and Winston, 1962. 274pp.

1934 *Indian Thought and Its Development.* Boston: Beacon Press, 1960. 272pp. Magnolia, Mass.: Peter Smith, 1962.

1936 "African Hunting Stories." In *The Animal World of Albert Schweitzer,* ed. by Charles R. Joy. Boston: Beacon Press, 1958. 209pp.

1938 *From My African Notebook.* Glouster, Mass.: Peter Smith, 1966. 144pp.

1949 *Das Spital im Urwald. (The Jungle Hospital)* Photographs by Anna Wildikann. Munich: C.H. Beck, 1950. 52pp.

1950 *A Pelican Tells About His Life.* New York: Hawthorn, 1965. 65pp.

1954 *The Problem of Peace in the World of Today.* New York: Harper, 1954. 19pp.

1958 *Peace or Atomic War?* New York: Henry Holt. Port Washington, New York: Kennikat Press, 1972. 47pp.

1963 *The Teaching of Reverence for Life.* New York: Holt, Rinehart and Winston, 1965. 63pp.

1967 *The Kingdom of God and Primitive Christianity.* New York: Seabury, 1968. 193pp.

B. BOOKS ABOUT ALBERT SCHWEITZER, Including Anthologies.

Anderson,Erica. *Albert Schweitzer's Gift of Friendship.* New York: Harper & Row, 1976. 142pp.

Anderson,Erica. *The Schweitzer Album, A Portrait in Works and Pictures.* New York: Harper & Row, 1965. 176pp.

Anderson, Erica and Eugene Exman. *The World of Albert Schweitzer. A Book of Photographs.* New York: Harper, 1955. 144pp.

Booth, Edwin Prince, *et al,* eds. *A Tribute on the Ninetieth Birthday of Albert Schweitzer.* Boston: Henry N. Sawyer, 1964. 96pp.

Brabazon, James. *Albert Schweitzer: A Biography.* New York: G. P. Putnam, 1975. 509pp.

Cousins, Norman. *Dr. Schweitzer of Lambaréné.* Westport, Conn.: Greenwood Press, 1973. 254pp.

Cousins, Norman. *The Words of Albert Schweitzer.* New York: Newmarket, 1984. 112pp.

Cousins, Norman. *Albert Schweitzer's Mission: Healing and Peace.* New York: W. W. Norton, 1985. 319pp.

Feschotte, Jacques. *Albert Schweitzer, An Introduction.* Boston: Beacon Press, 1955. 130pp.

Gollomb, Joseph. *Albert Schweitzer: Genius in the Jungle.* New York: Vanguard Press, 1949. 249pp.

Griffith, Nancy S. and Laura Person. *Albert Schweitzer: An International Bibliography.* Boston: G. K. Hall, 1981. 600pp.

Hagedorn, Hermann. *Albert Schweitzer: Prophet in the Wilderness.* New York: Collier Books, 1962. 224pp.

Jack, Homer A. ed.*To Albert Schweitzer: A Festschrift Commemorating His 80th Birthday. . .*Evanston, Ill.: Privately printed, 1955. 178pp.

Joy, Charles R. *Albert Schweitzer: An Anthology.* Boston: Beacon Press, 1947. 323pp. Revised and enlarged, 1965. 367pp. 1977.

Joy, Charles R. and Melvin Arnold. *The Africa of Albert Schweitzer.* New York: Harper. Boston: Beacon Press, 1948. 160pp.

Joy, Charles R., ed. *The Wit and Wisdom of Albert Schweitzer.* Boston: Beacon Press, 1949. 104pp.

Joy, Charles R. ed. *The Animal World of Albert Schweitzer: Jungle Insights into Reverence for Life.* Boston: Beacon Press, 1950. 207pp.

Joy, Charles R., ed. *Music in the Life of Albert Schweitzer.* New York: Harper. Boston: Beacon Press, 1951. 300pp. Freeport, N.Y.: Books for Libraries Press, 1971.

Kiernan, Thomas. *A Treasury of Albert Schweitzer.* Salem, N.H.: Ayer Co, 1965.

Marshall, George N. and David Poling. *Schweitzer: A Biography.* Garden City, N.Y.: Doubleday, 1971. 342pp.

McKnight, Gerald. *Verdict on Schweitzer, The Man Behind the Legend of Lambaréné.* New York: John Day, 1964. 254pp.

Mozley, E. N. *The Theology of Albert Schweitzer for Christian Inquirers.* New York: Gordon Press, 1977. 117pp.

Payne, Pierre Stephen Robert. *The Three Worlds of Albert Schweitzer.* Bloomington, Indiana: Indiana University Press, 1961. 252pp.

Ratter, Magnus. *Albert Schweitzer, Life and Message.* Boston: Beacon Press, 1950. 214pp.

Reginald, H., ed. *Reverence for Life.* New York: Irvington, 1980. New York: Pilgrim, 1980.

Roback, A. A., ed. *The Albert Schweitzer Jubilee Book.* Cambridge, Mass.: Sci-Art Publishers, 1945. 508pp.

Roback, A. A., ed. *In Albert Schweitzer's Realms: A Symposium.* Cambridge, Mass.: Sci-Art Publishers, 1962. 441pp.

Regester, John Dickinson. *Albert Schweitzer, The Man and His Work.* New York: Abingdon Press, 1931. 145pp.

Seaver, George. *Albert Schweitzer, the Man and His Mind.* New York: Harper, Sixth definitive edition 1969. 365pp.

## C. WRITINGS BY ALBERT SCHWEITZER ON PEACE

1. Peace Prize Address in Frankfurt. (1951)
   "Speech on Albert Schweitzer; The Man and His Way for Mankind." *Universitas.* English language edition. 7:1 (1964). pp.19–24.
2. Letter to *Daily Herald,* London. (1954)
   "The H-Bomb." *Daily Herald.* April 11, 1954, p. 4.
   *Saturday Review* (July 17, 1954), p. 23.
   *Science* Sept. 10, 1954, p. 11a.
   *Science Monthly* (October 1954), p. 208.
   *Bulletin of the Atomic Scientists* (November 1954), p. 339.
3. Nobel Peace Prize Address in Oslo. (1954)
   "The Problem of Peace in the World of Today." New York: Harper, 1954. 19pp. London: A. and C. Black, 1954. 20pp.
   Haberman, Frederick W., ed. *Peace 1951–1970: Nobel Lectures, including Presentation Speeches and Laureates' Biographies.* Amsterdam, London, New York: Elsevier, 1972. vol. III. pp. 46–57.
   *Christian Register* (January 1955), pp. 11–15.
4. A Declaration of Conscience, Radio Oslo. (1957)
   *Saturday Review* (May 18, 1957), pp. 17–20.
   *Bulletin of the Atomic Scientists* (June 1957), pp. 204–205.

Pauling, Linus. *No More War!* New York: Dodd, Mead, 1958. pp. 225-237.

*The Reporter,* (May 16, 1957), p. 26.

5. Peace or Atomic War? Radio Oslo. (1958)

*Peace or Atomic War?* New York: Henry Holt, 1958. 47pp. London: A. and C. Black, 1958. 47pp. Port Washington, N.Y.: Kennikat Press, 1972. 47pp.

BOOKS AND ARTICLES ABOUT ALBERT SCHWEITZER'S PEACE TESTIMONY.

Cousins, Norman. "The Schweitzer Declaration." *The Saturday Review,* May 18, 1957, pp. 13-16.

Cousins, Norman. "An Open Letter to David Lawrence." *The Saturday Review,* July 6, 1957, pp. 20-21.

Cousins, Norman. "Mr. Cousins' Comments on Dr. Schweitzer's Stand," *U.S. News and World Report,* August 2, 1957, p. 90.

Cousins, Norman. *Dr. Schweitzer of Lambaréné.* New York: New York: Harper, 1960. 254pp.

Cousins, Norman. *Albert Schweitzer's Mission; Healing and Peace.* New York: W. W. Norton, 1985. 319pp.

Hojer, Signe. "Schweitzer Speaks to Peace Workers." *The American Friend.* 46:14, p. 210.

Jack, Homer A. "The Same First Name." *The Courier,* Summer 1986, pp. 5-9.

Libby, Willard F. "An Open Letter to Dr. Schweitzer." *The Saturday Review,* May 25, 1957, pp. 8-9.

Schweitzer, Albert. "I Have One Wish" *Newsweek,* May 16, 1960, p. 78.

Spiegelberg, Herbert ed., "The Correspondence Between Bertrand Russell and Albert Schweitzer, *International Studies in Philosophy,* vol. 12. (1980).

Tau, Max. *Albert Schweitzer und der Friede.* Hamburg: Meiner, 1955. 32pp.

Winnubst, Benedictus. *Das Friedensdenken Albert Schweitzers.* Amsterdam: Rodopi, 1974. 219pp.

"To The Men of Geneva." *The Saturday Review,* Nov. 22, 1958, p. 22.

"Dr. Schweitzer Stirs World Conscience." *The Christian Century,* May 8, 1957, pp. 579-580.

# Index